SACRE MOMENTS

E-Z Play Today 75 — For Organs, Pianos & Electronic Keyboards

Contents

2	Amazing Grace
4	And Can It Be That I Should Gain
6	Blessed Assurance
8	Blessing And Honor
10	Bring Them In
12	Fairest Lord Jesus
14	Father, We Come To Thee
16	God Himself Is With Us
38	Have You Any Room For Jesus?
18	How Beauteous Were The Marks Divine
20	I Love To Tell The Story
22	I Need Thee Every Hour
24	I Sing The Mighty Pow'r Of God
26	I Surrender All
28	I'll Live For Him
30	Love Lifted Me
32	Nearer, My God, To Thee
34	Oh, How I Love Jesus
36	On Christ, The Solid Rock, I Stand
41	Praise God, From Whom All Blessings Flow
42	Praise To God, Immortal Praise
44	Rise Up, Oh Men Of God
46	Rock Of Ages
48	Send The Light
54	Tell Me The Old, Old Story
51	There Is Power In The Blood
56	'Tis So Sweet To Trust In Jesus
58	What A Friend We Have In Jesus
60	While Thee I Seek, Protecting Power
62	Wonderful Words Of Life
64	REGISTRATION GUIDE

ISBN 0-7935-0541-0

Hal Leonard Publishing Corporation
7777 West Bluemound Road   P.O. Box 13819   Milwaukee, WI 53213

E-Z Play ® TODAY Music Notation © 1975 HAL LEONARD PUBLISHING CORPORATION
Copyright © 1991 by HAL LEONARD PUBLISHING CORPORATION
International Copyright Secured   All Rights Reserved

For all works contained herein:
Unauthorized copying, arranging, adapting, recording or public performance is an infringement of copyright.
Infringers are liable under the law.

E-Z PLAY and EASY ELECTRONIC KEYBOARD MUSIC are registered trademarks of HAL LEONARD PUBLISHING CORPORATION.

Amazing Grace

Registration 2
Rhythm: Waltz

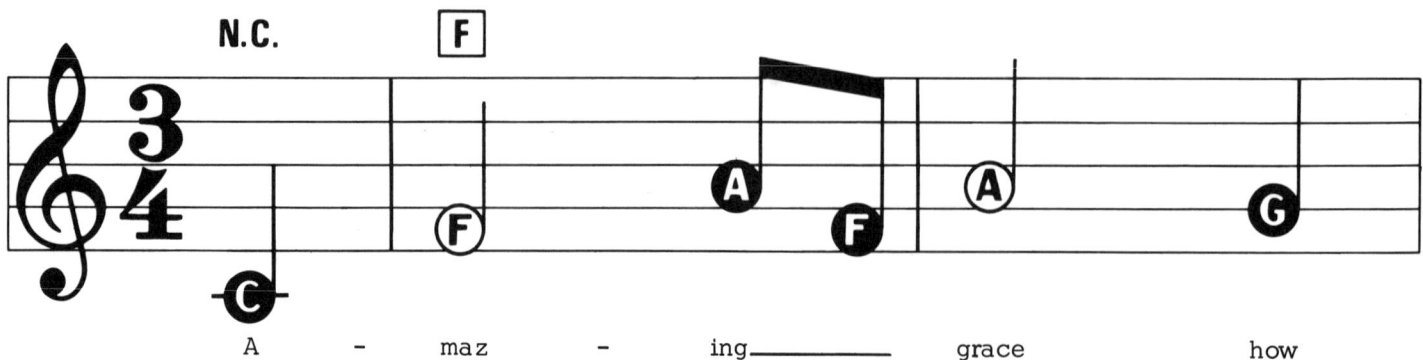
A - maz - ing grace how

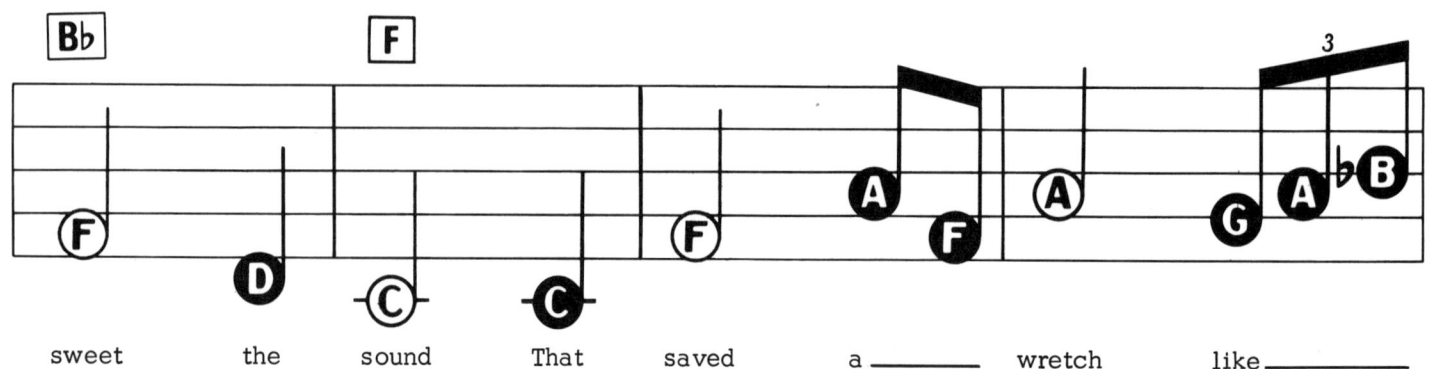
sweet the sound That saved a wretch like

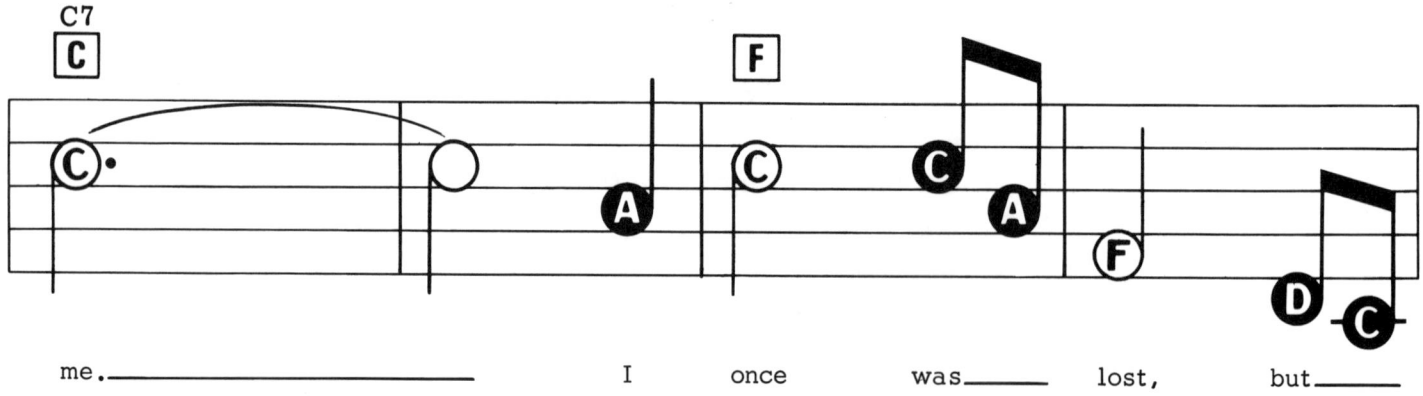
me. I once was lost, but

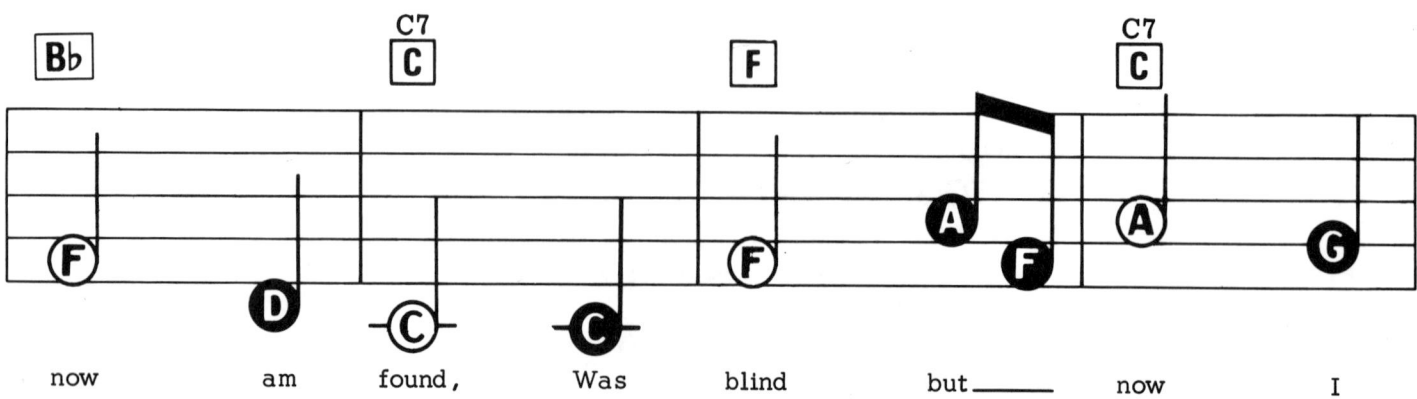
now am found, Was blind but now I

Copyright © 1991 by HAL LEONARD PUBLISHING CORPORATION
International Copyright Secured   All Rights Reserved

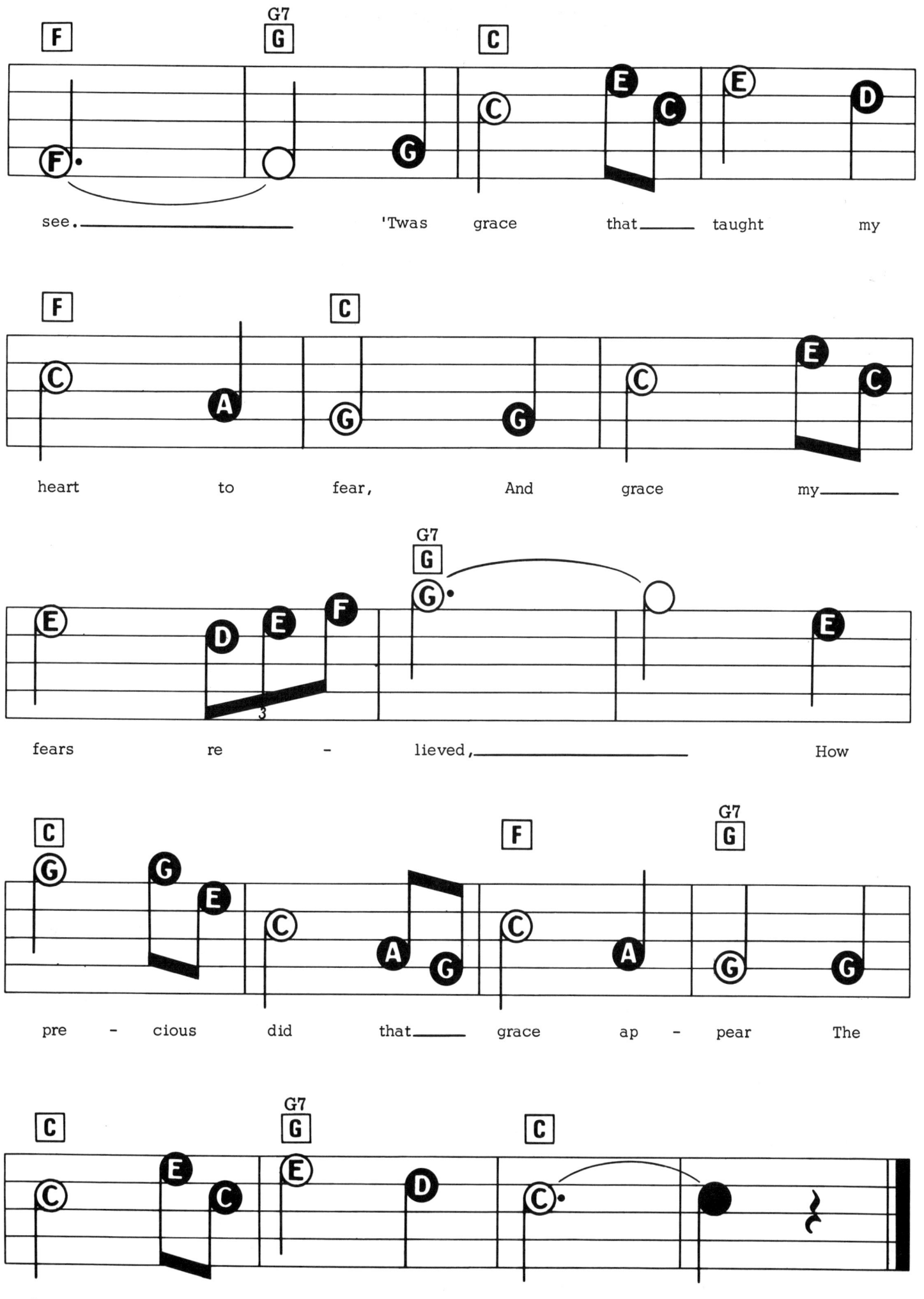

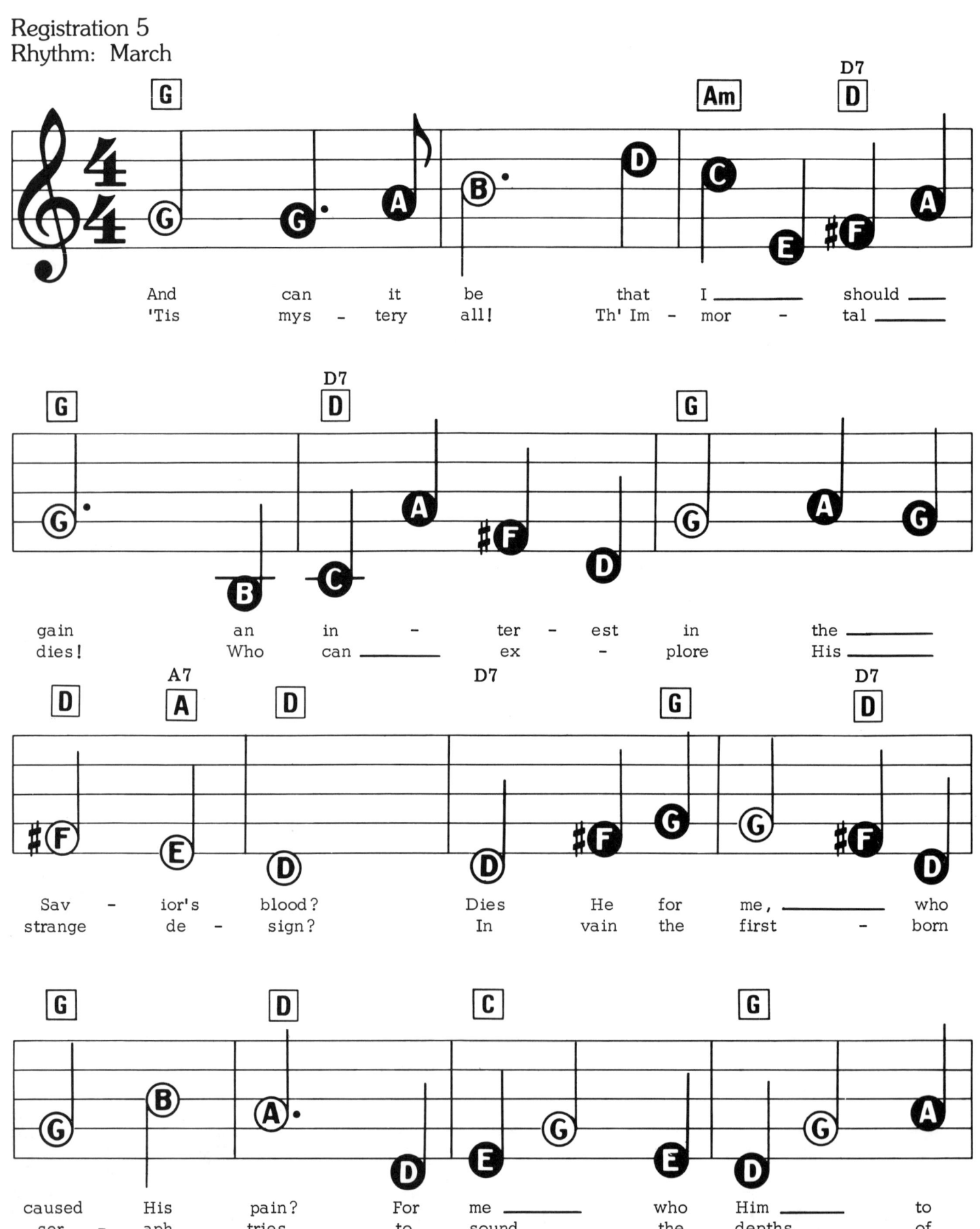

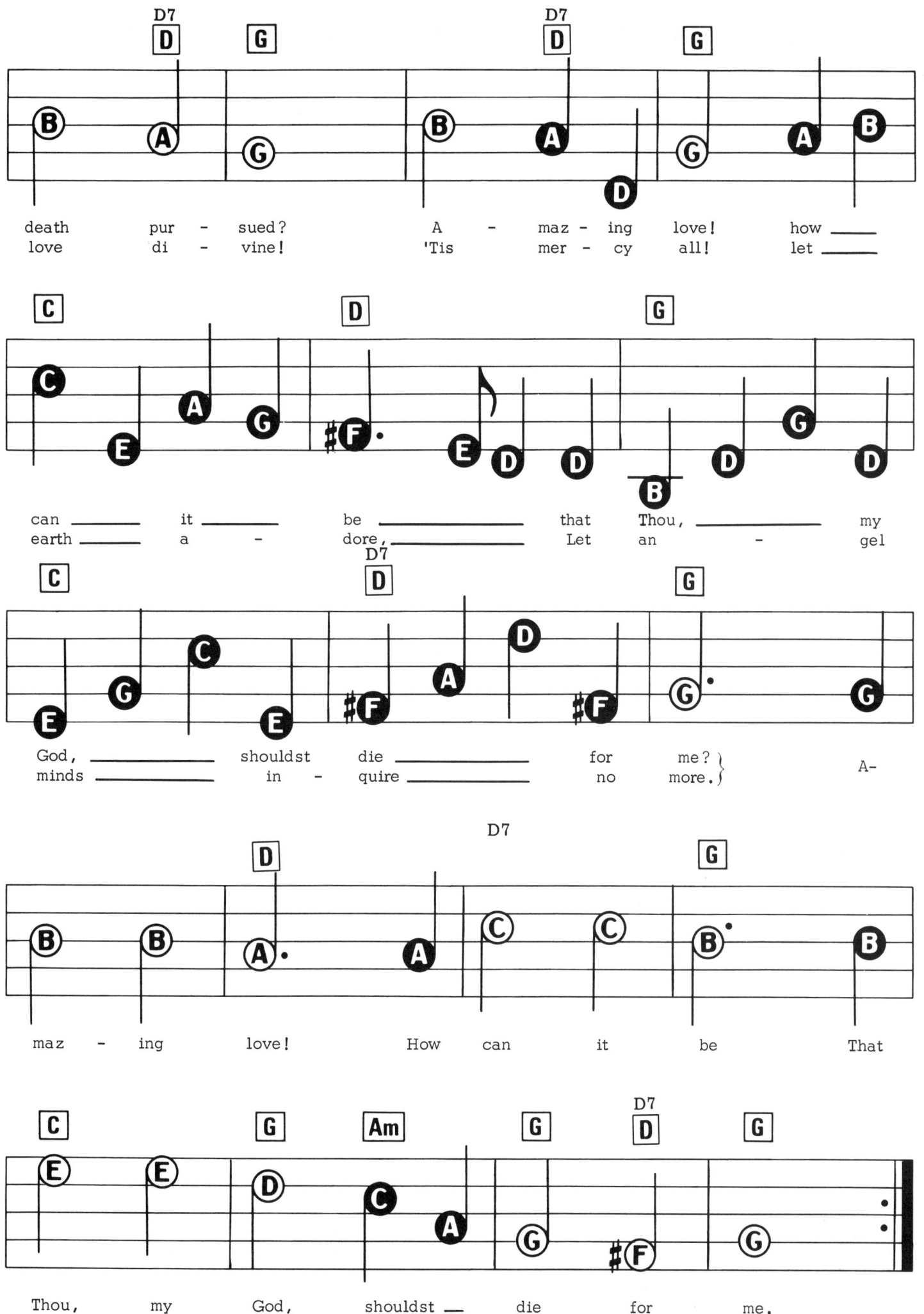

Blessed Assurance

Registration 6
Rhythm: Waltz

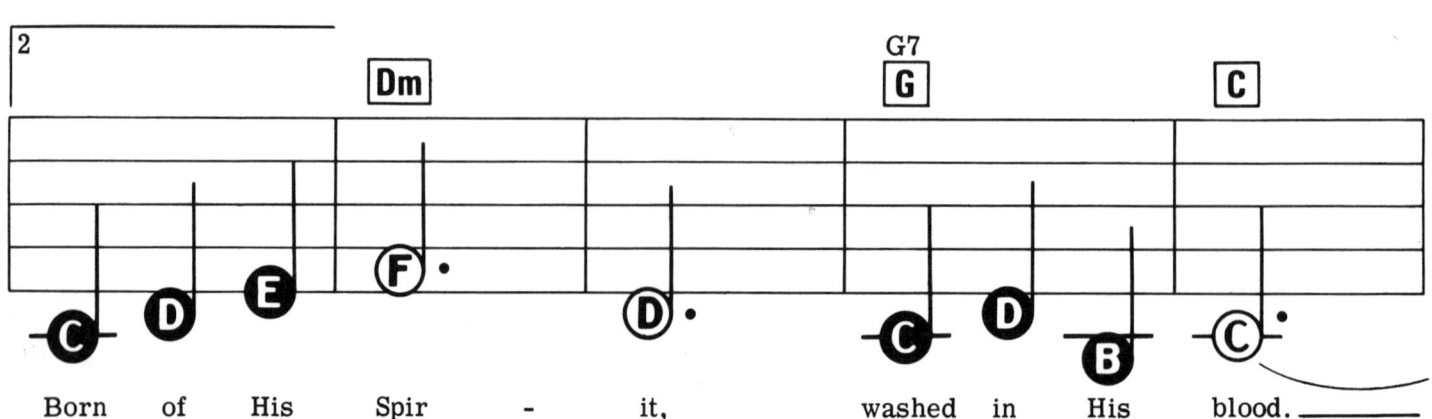

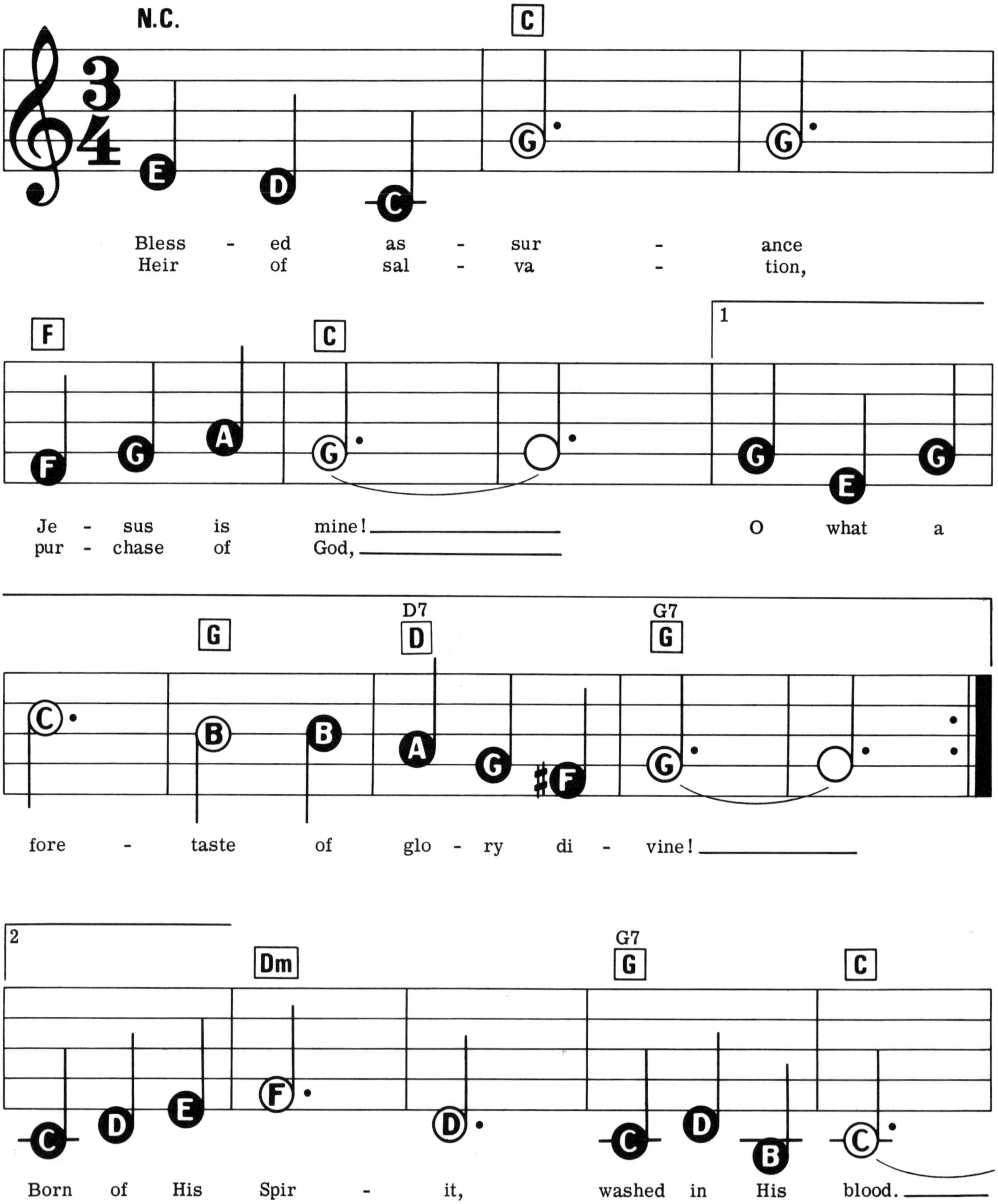

Blessed assurance, Jesus is mine!
Heir of salvation, purchase of God,

O what a foretaste of glory divine!

Born of His Spirit, washed in His blood.

Copyright © 1991 by HAL LEONARD PUBLISHING CORPORATION
International Copyright Secured   All Rights Reserved

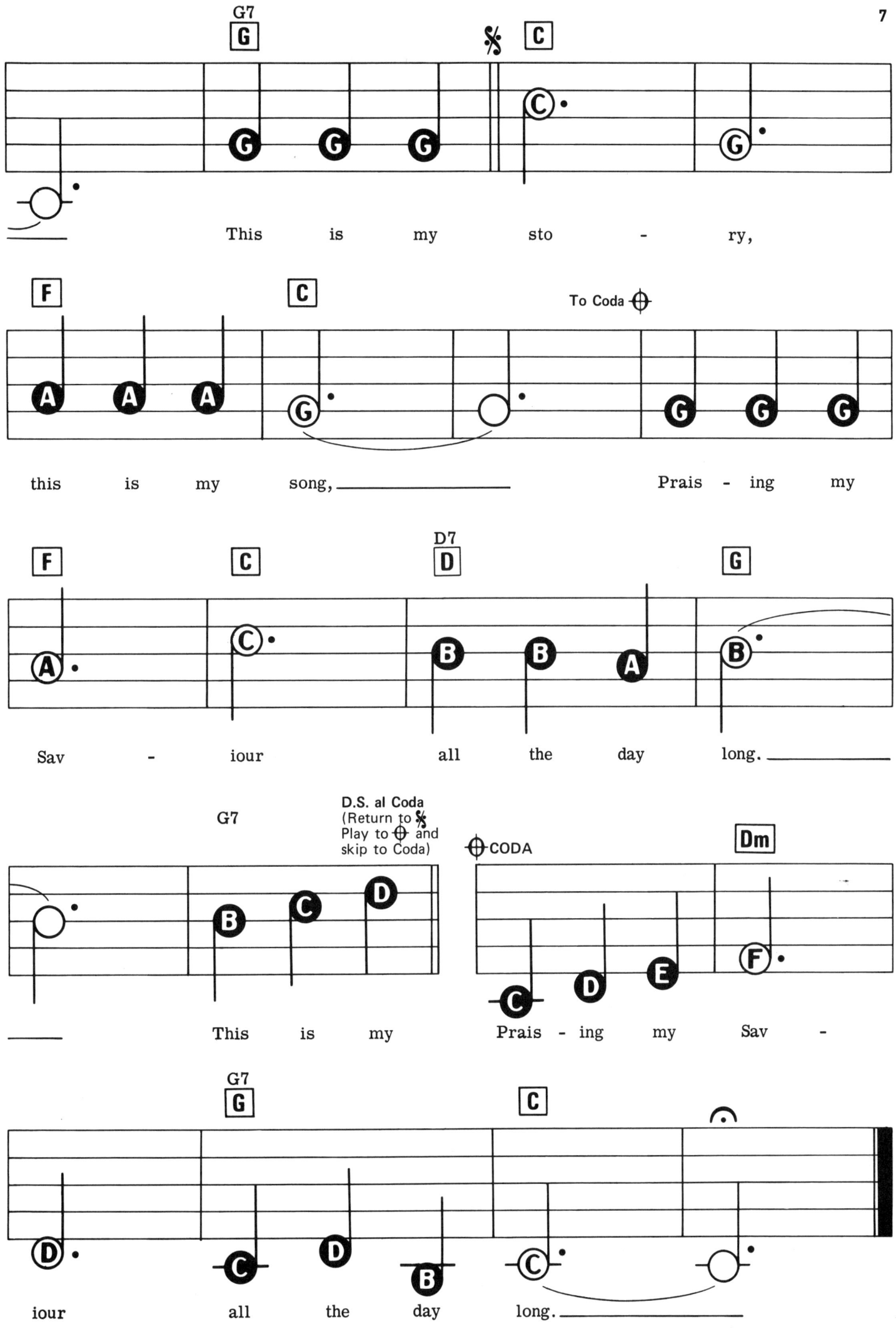

Blessing And Honor

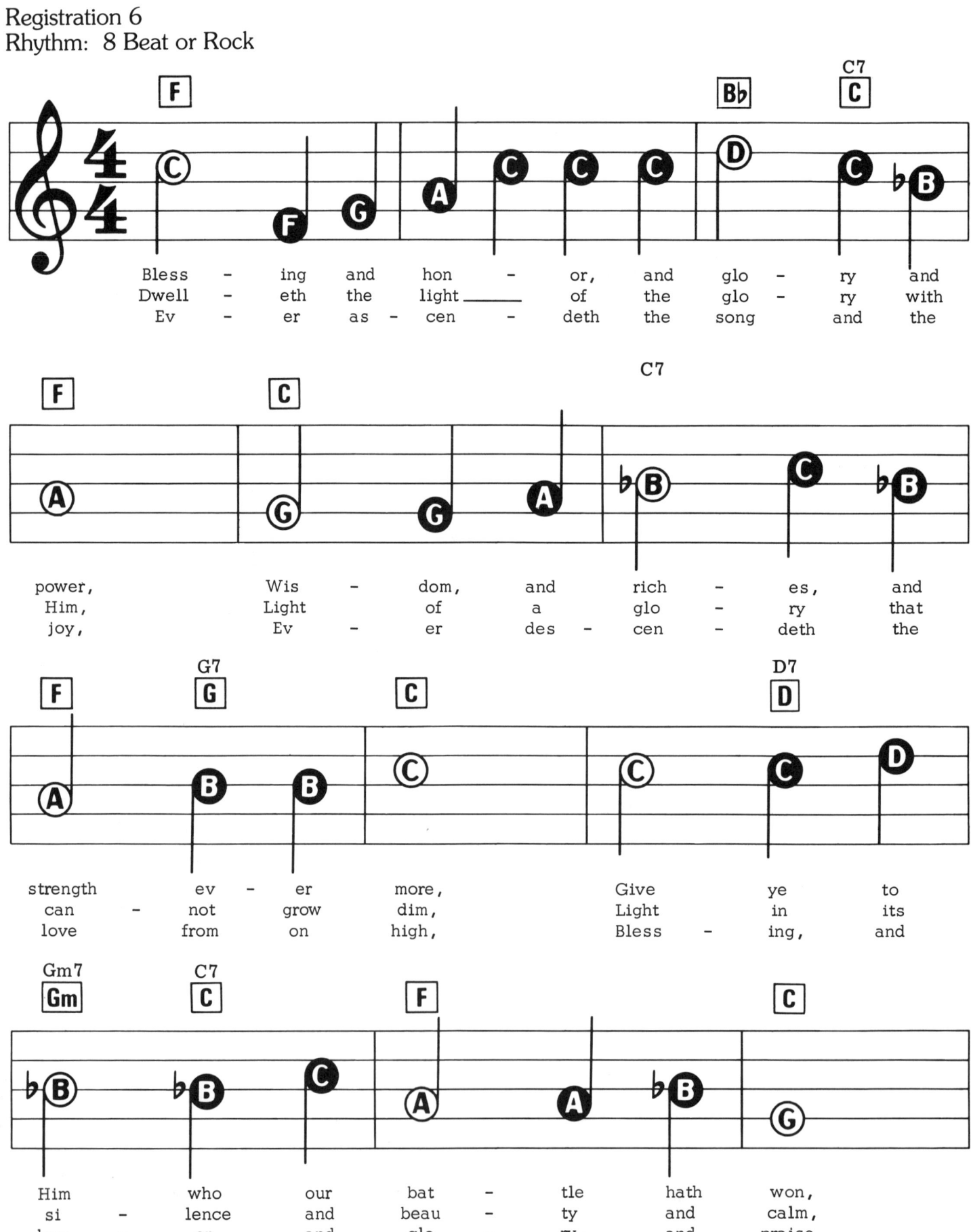

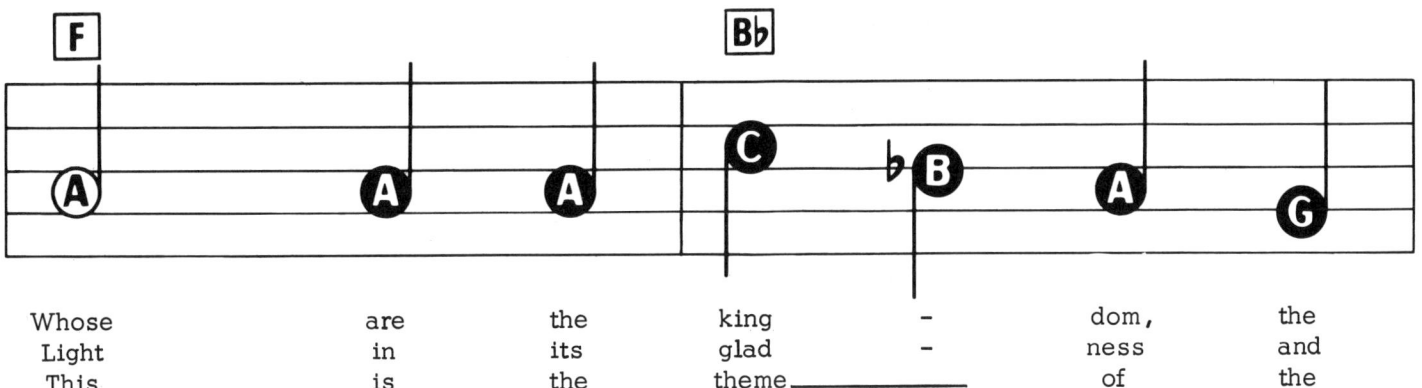
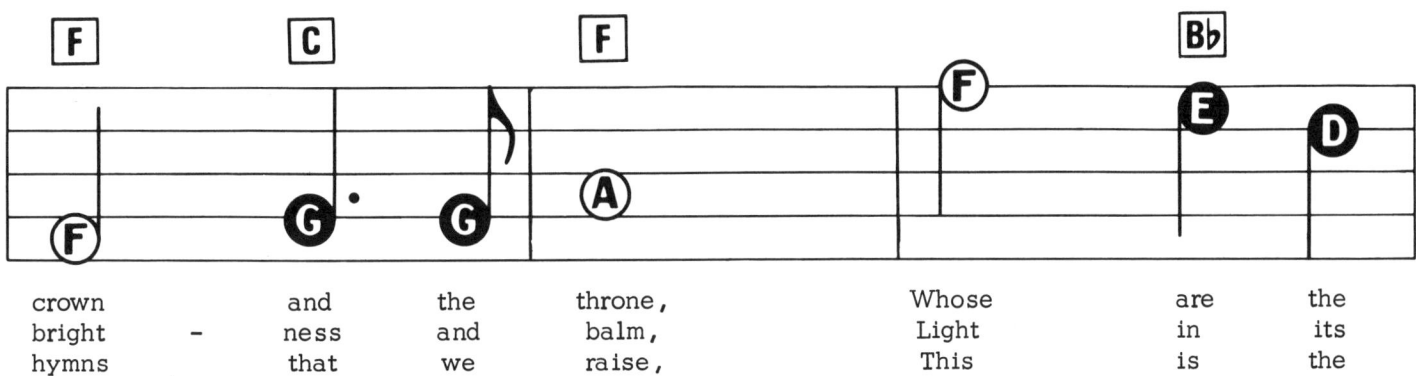
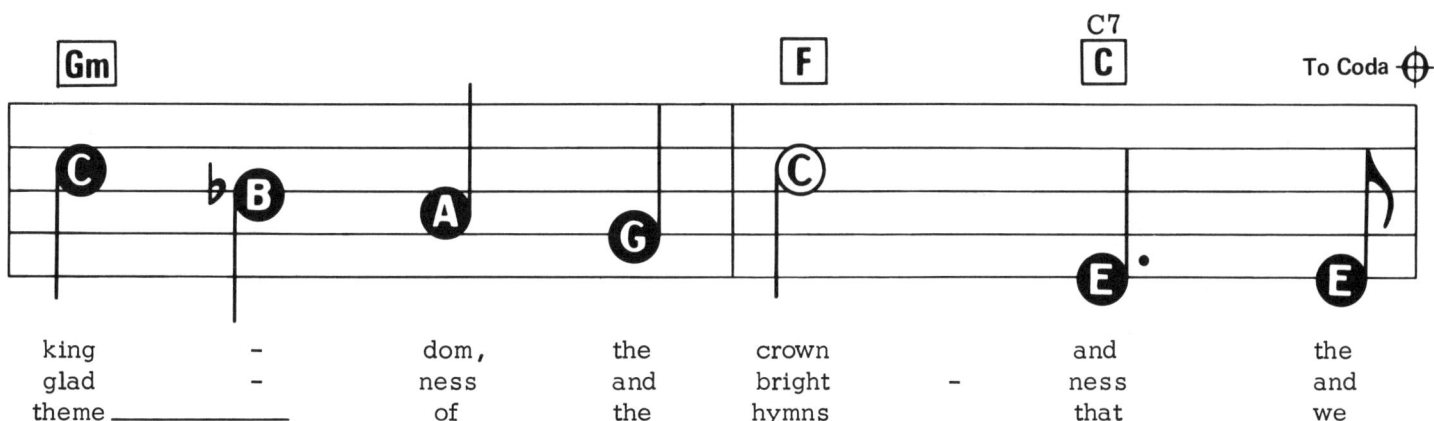
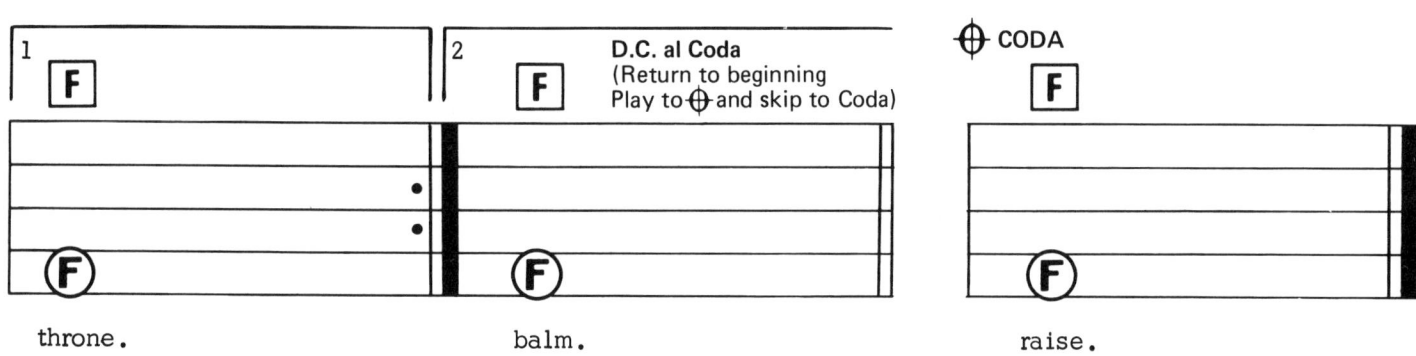

Bring Them In

Registration 3
Rhythm: 6/8 March

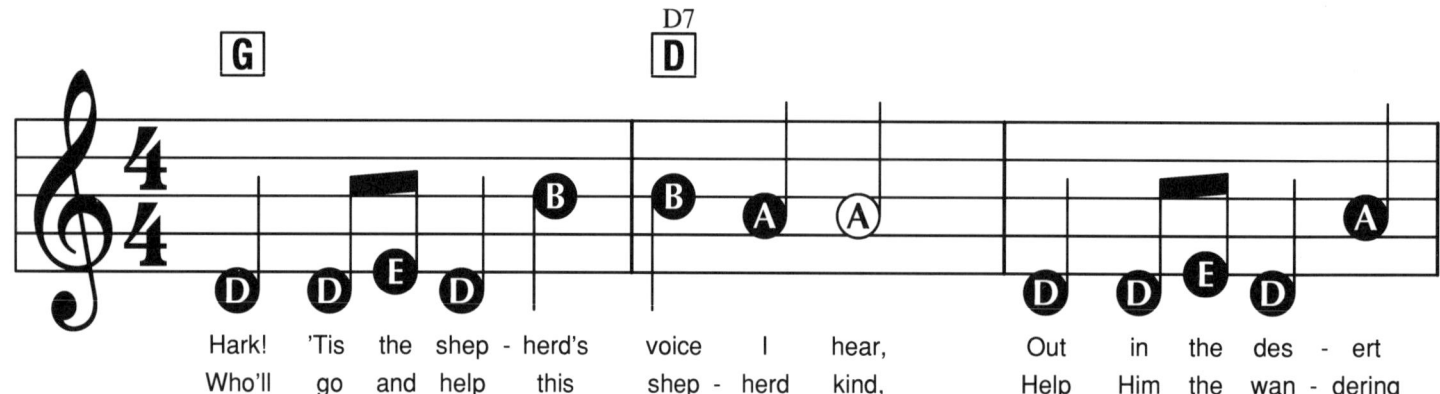
Hark! 'Tis the shep-herd's voice I hear, Out in the des - ert
Who'll go and help this shep-herd kind,

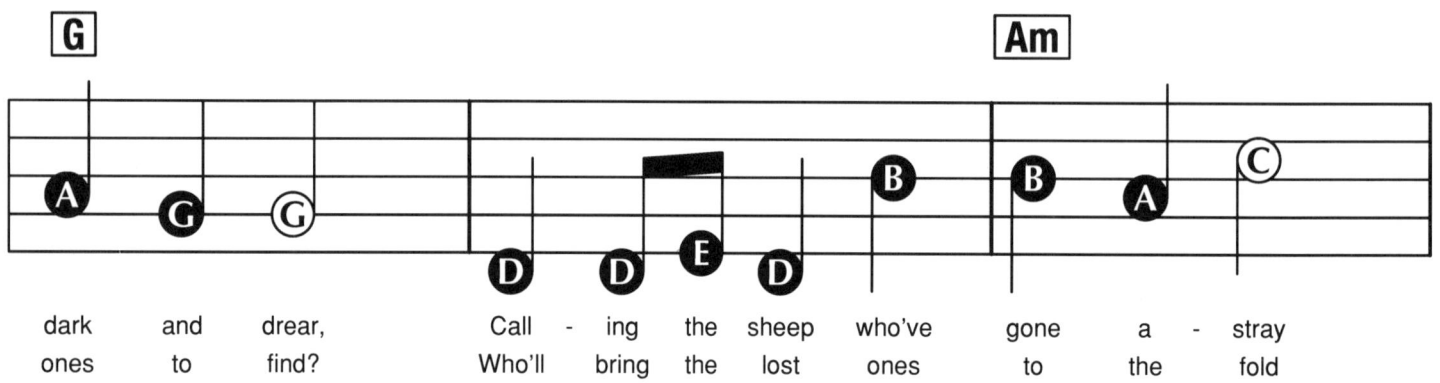
dark and drear, Call - ing the sheep who've gone a - stray
ones to find? Who'll bring the lost ones to the fold

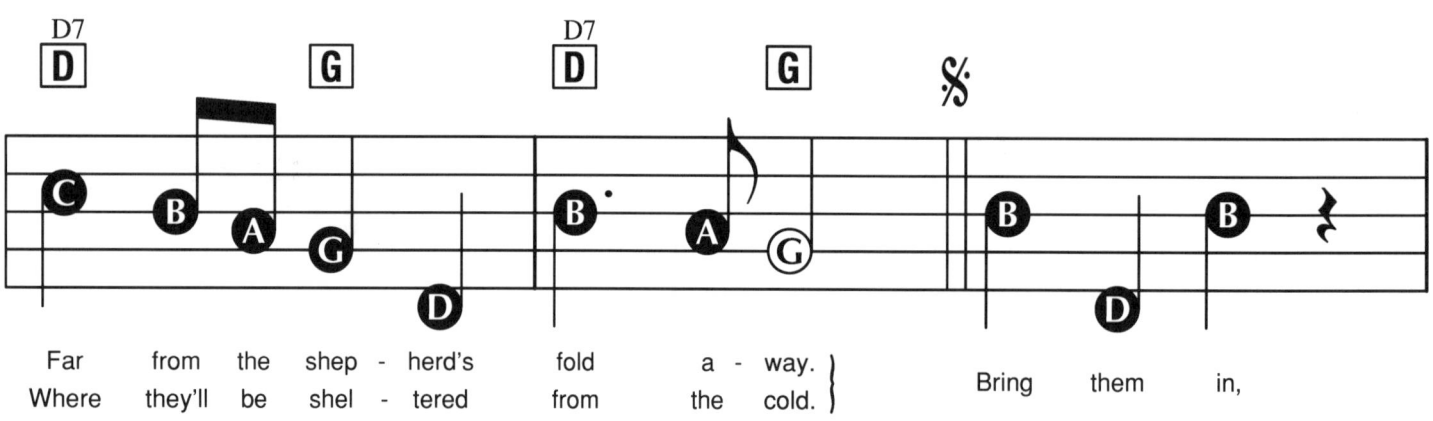
Far from the shep - herd's fold a - way.
Where they'll be shel - tered from the cold.
Bring them in,

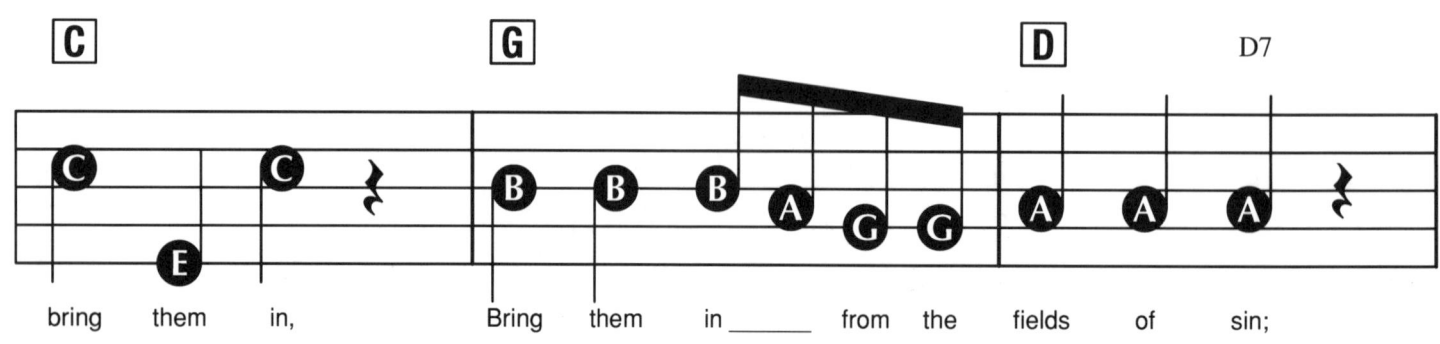
bring them in, Bring them in _____ from the fields of sin;

Copyright © 1991 by HAL LEONARD PUBLISHING CORPORATION
International Copyright Secured   All Rights Reserved

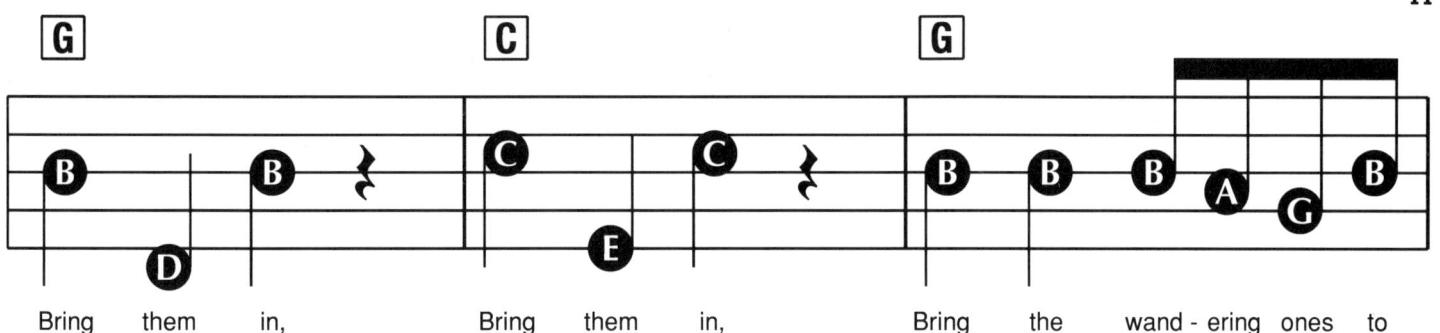
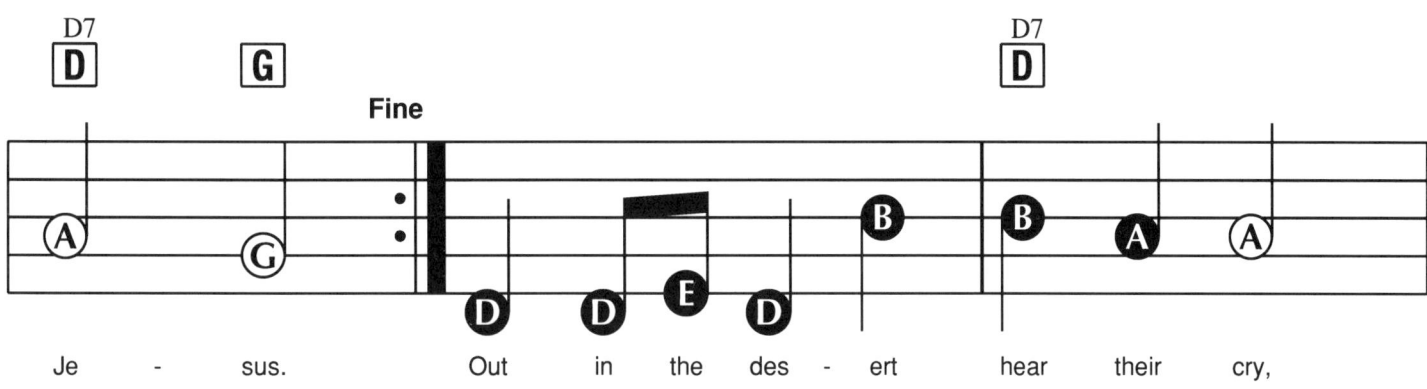
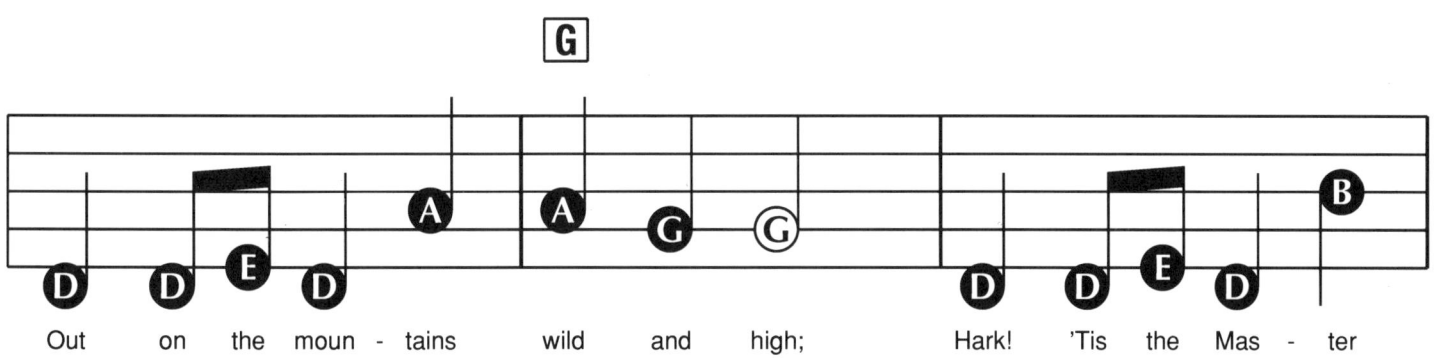
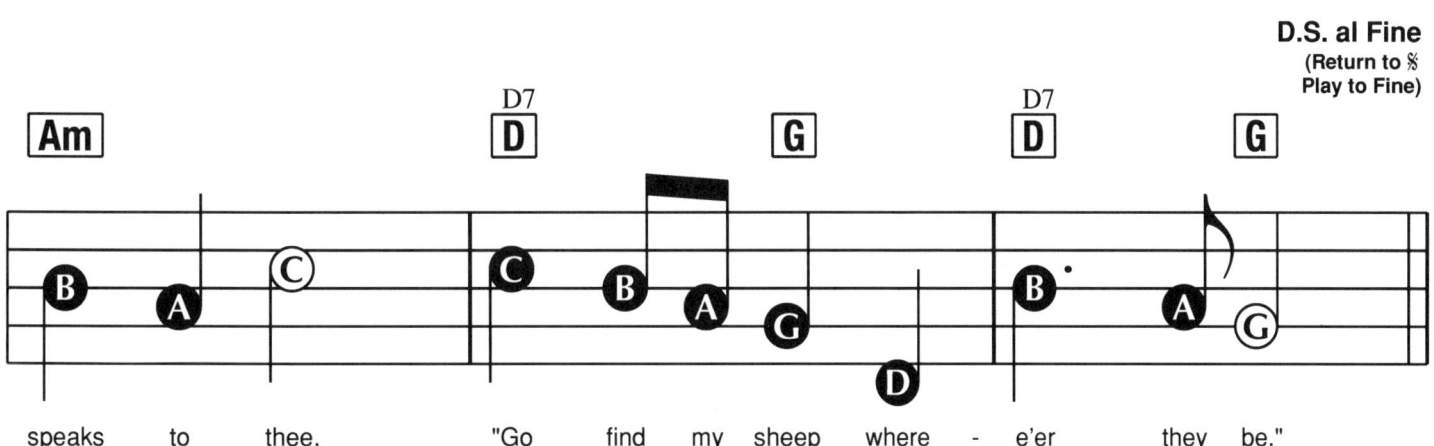

Fairest Lord Jesus

Registration 5
Rhythm: 8 Beat

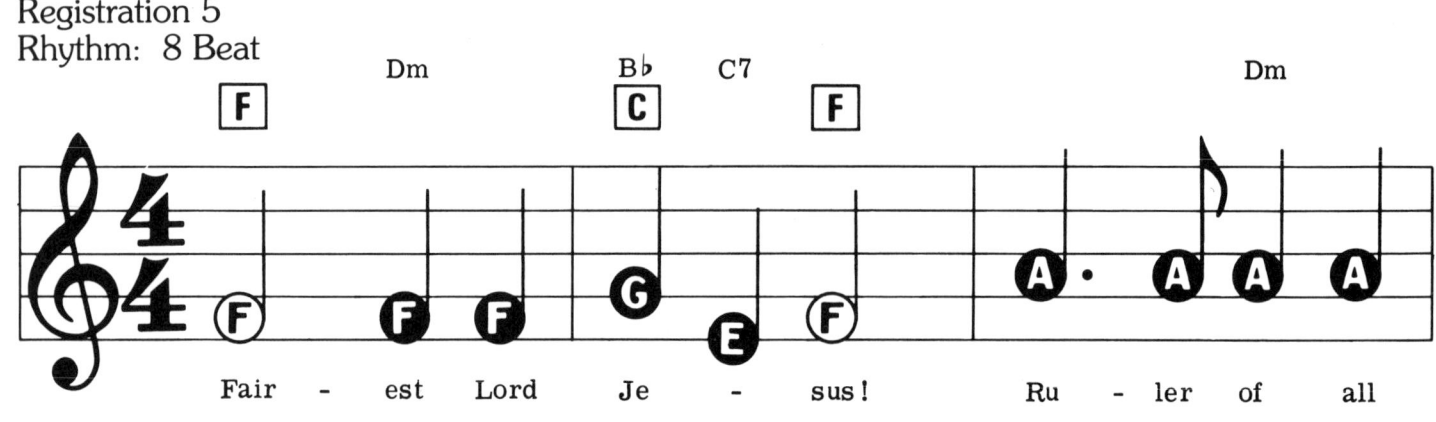

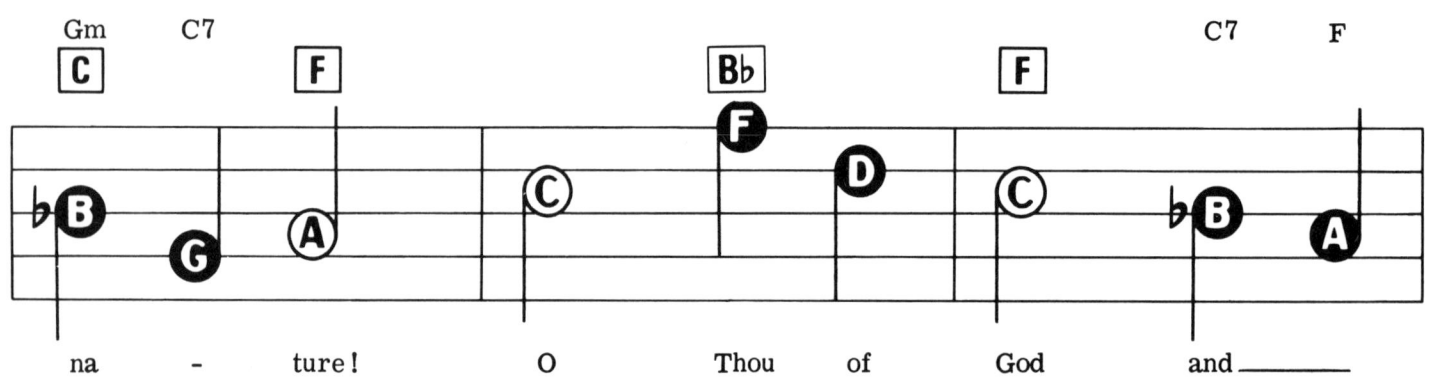

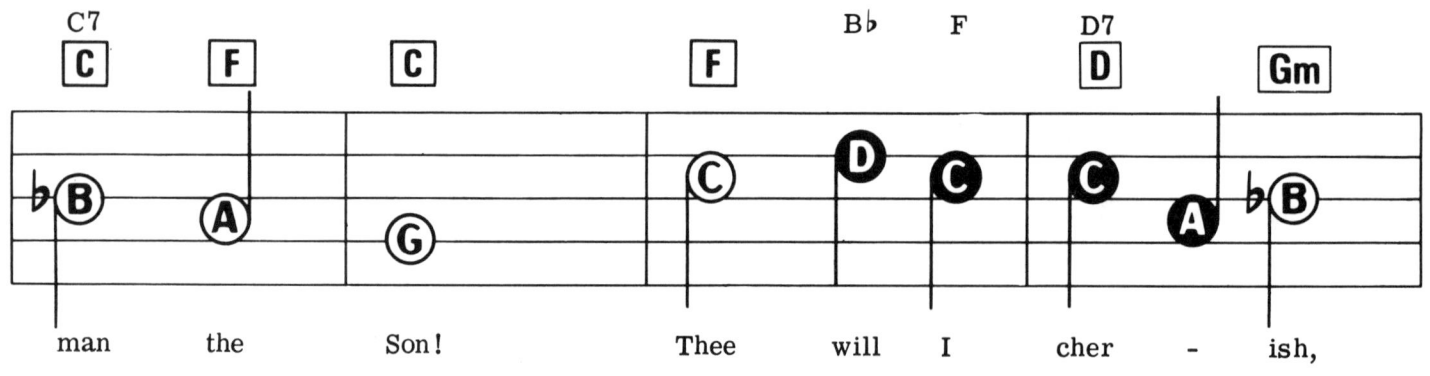

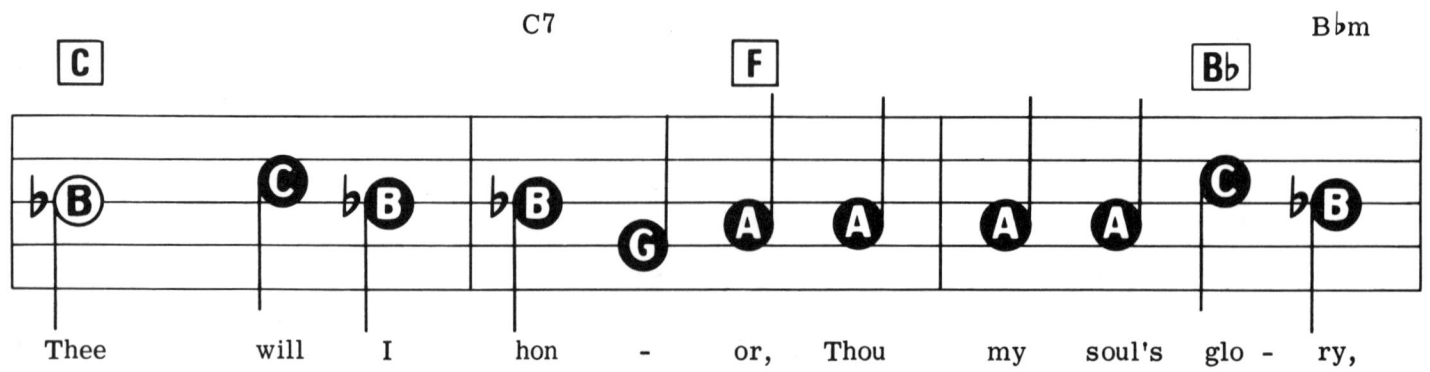

Copyright © 1991 by HAL LEONARD PUBLISHING CORPORATION
International Copyright Secured   All Rights Reserved

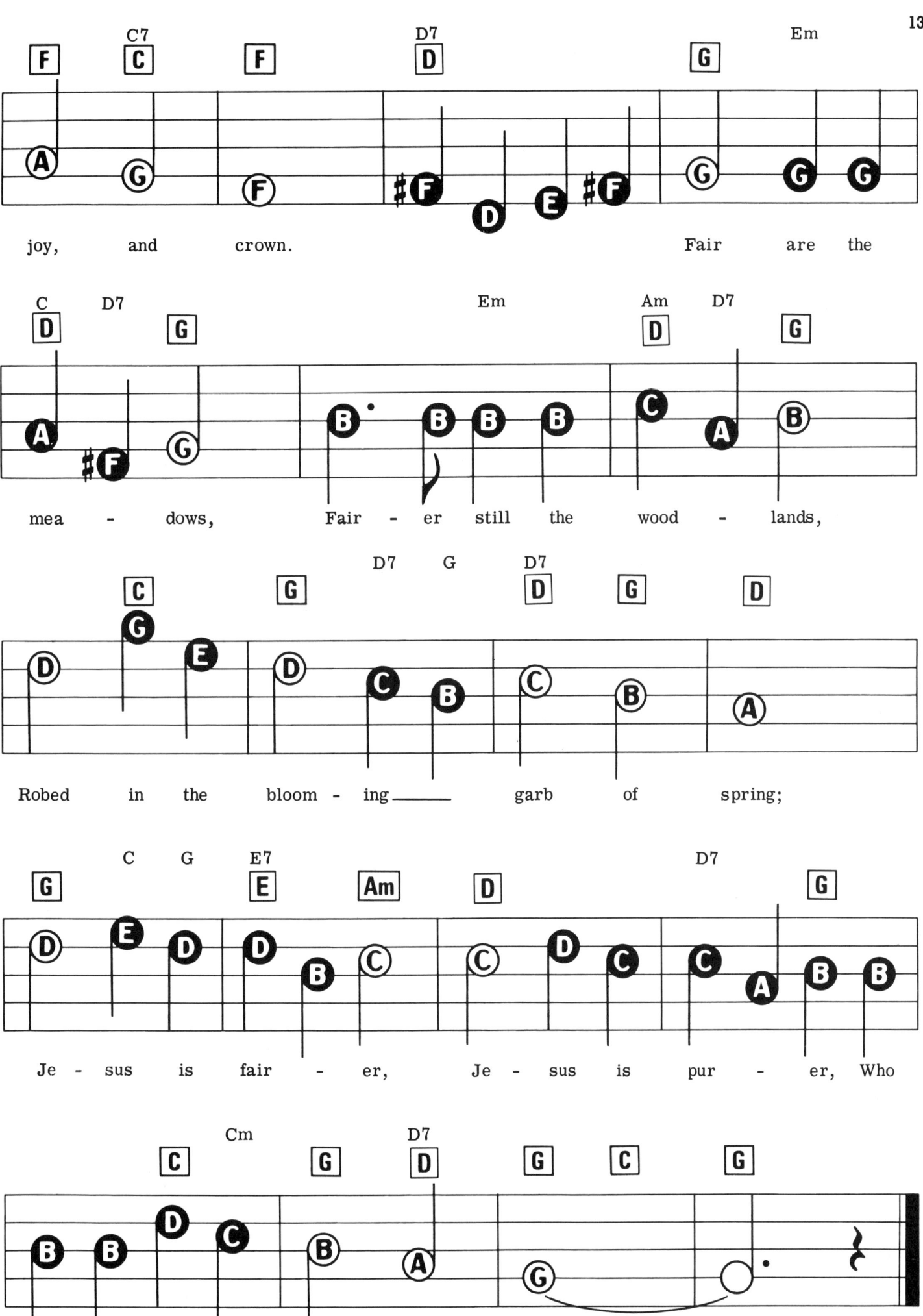

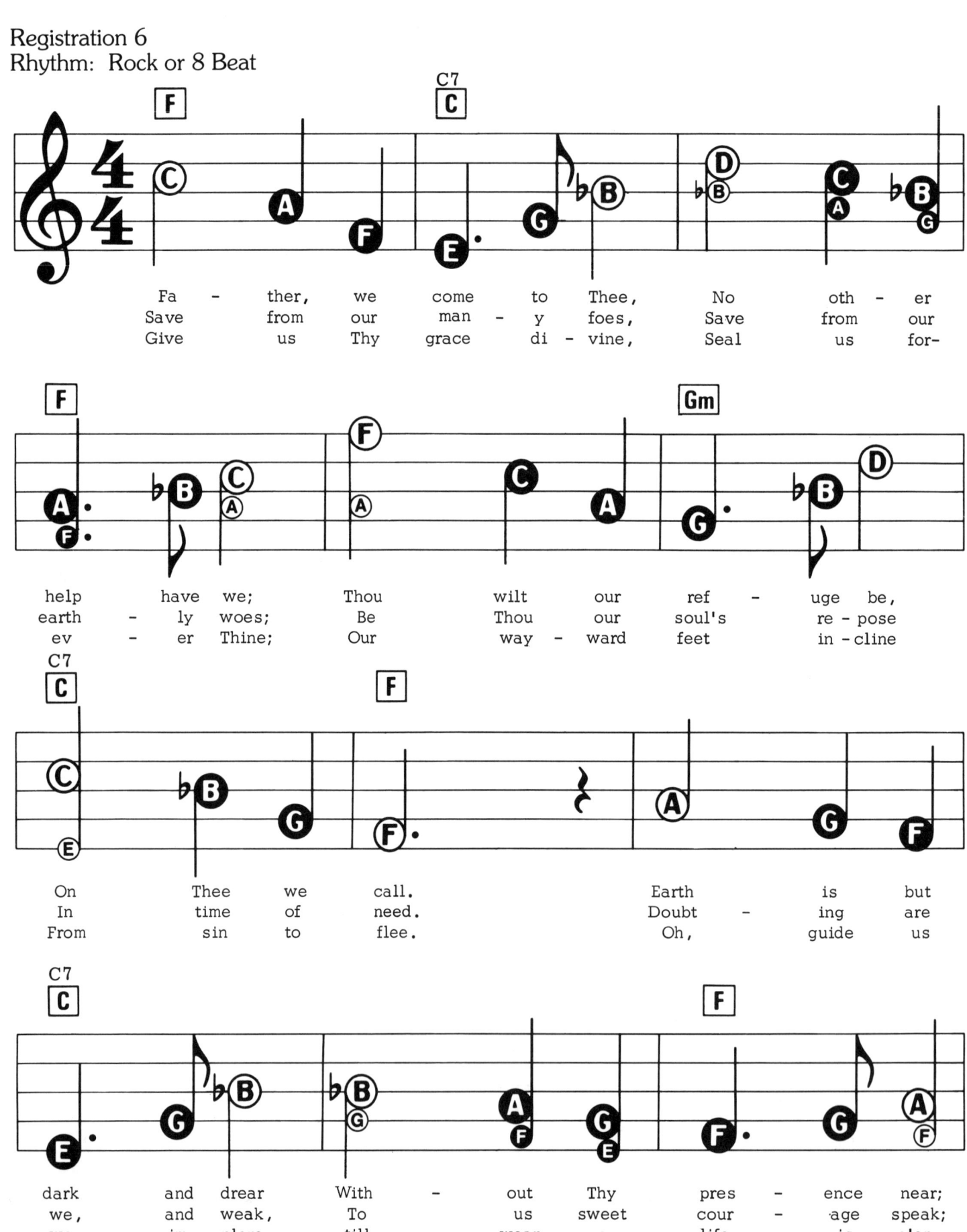

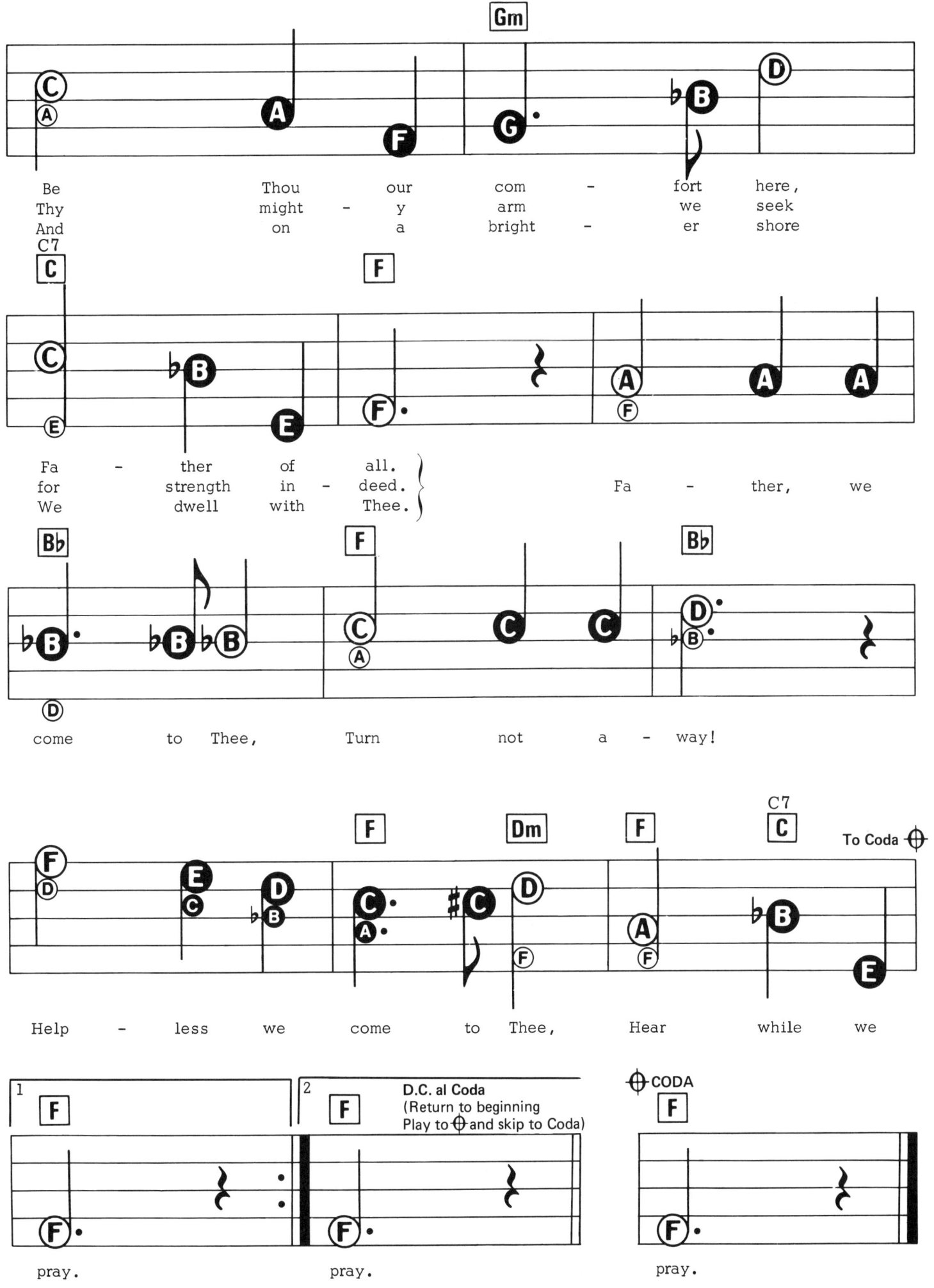

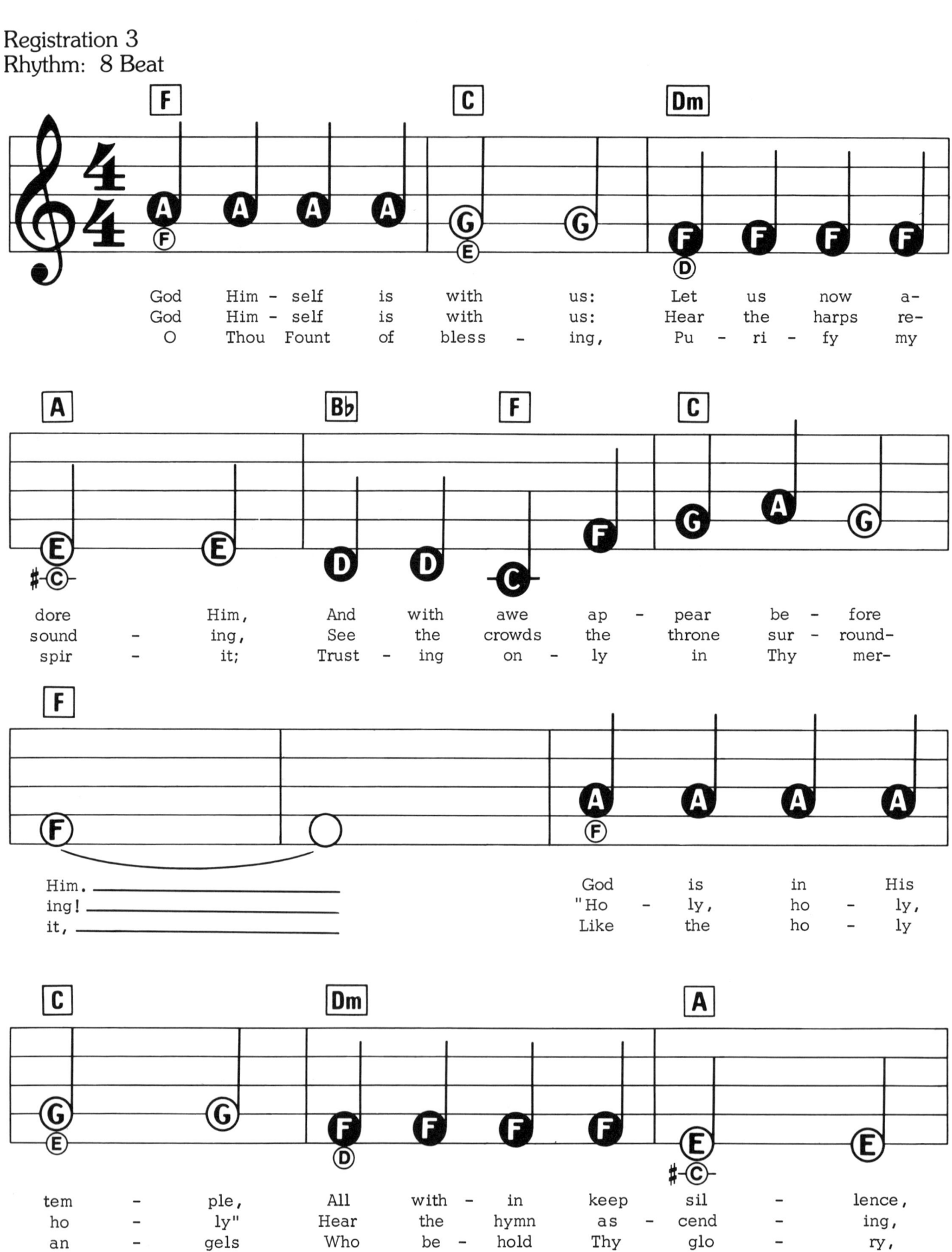

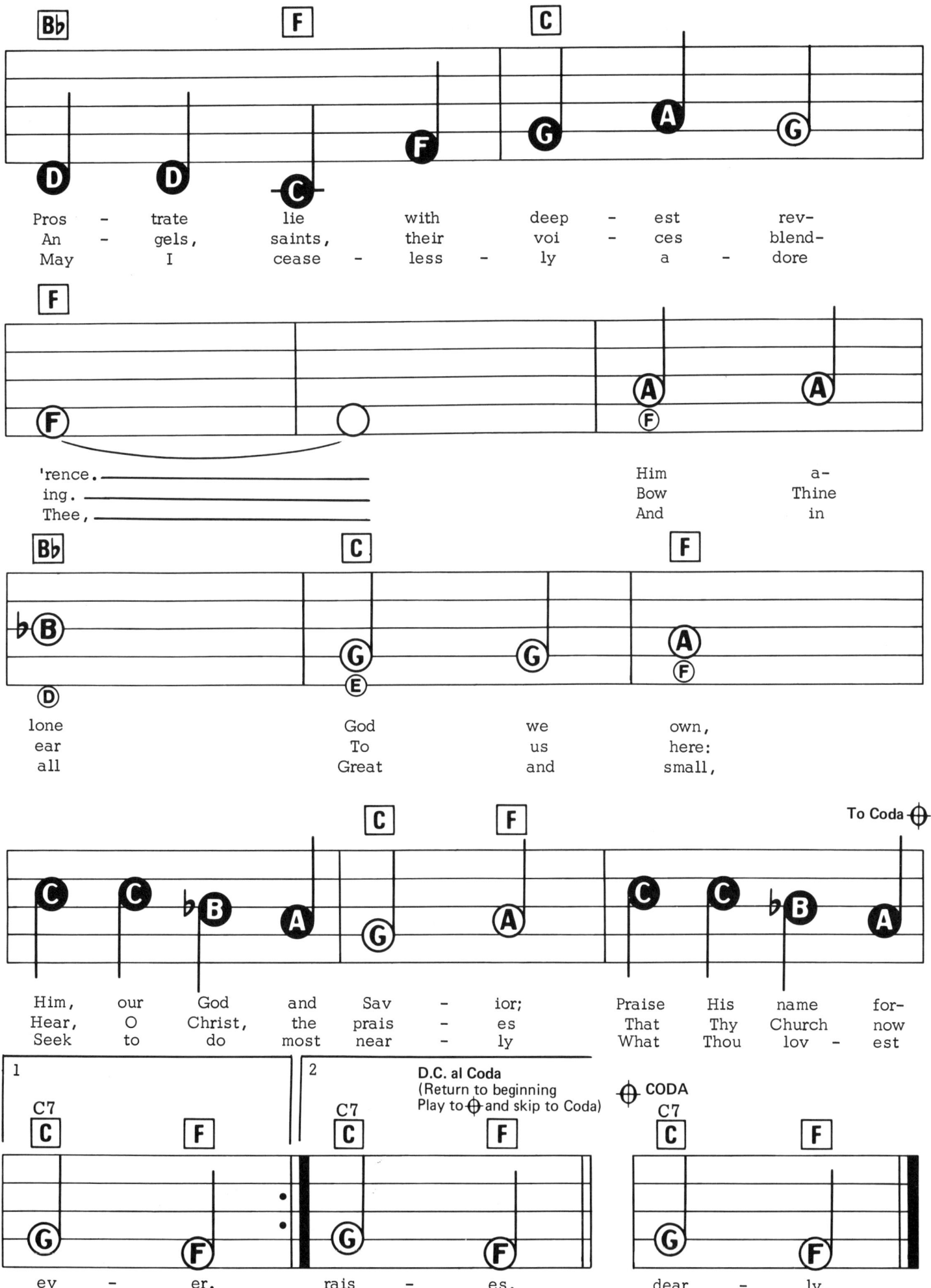

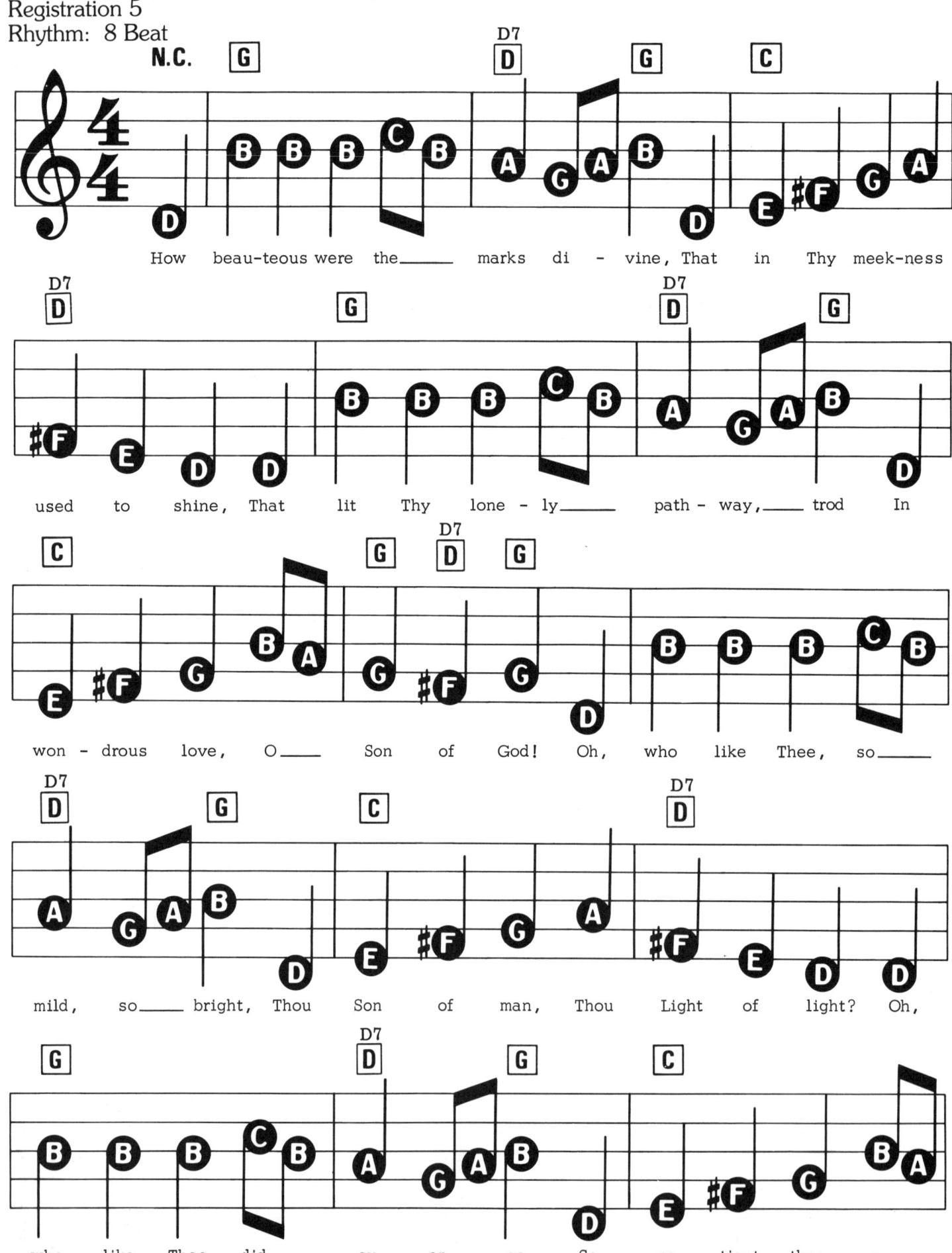

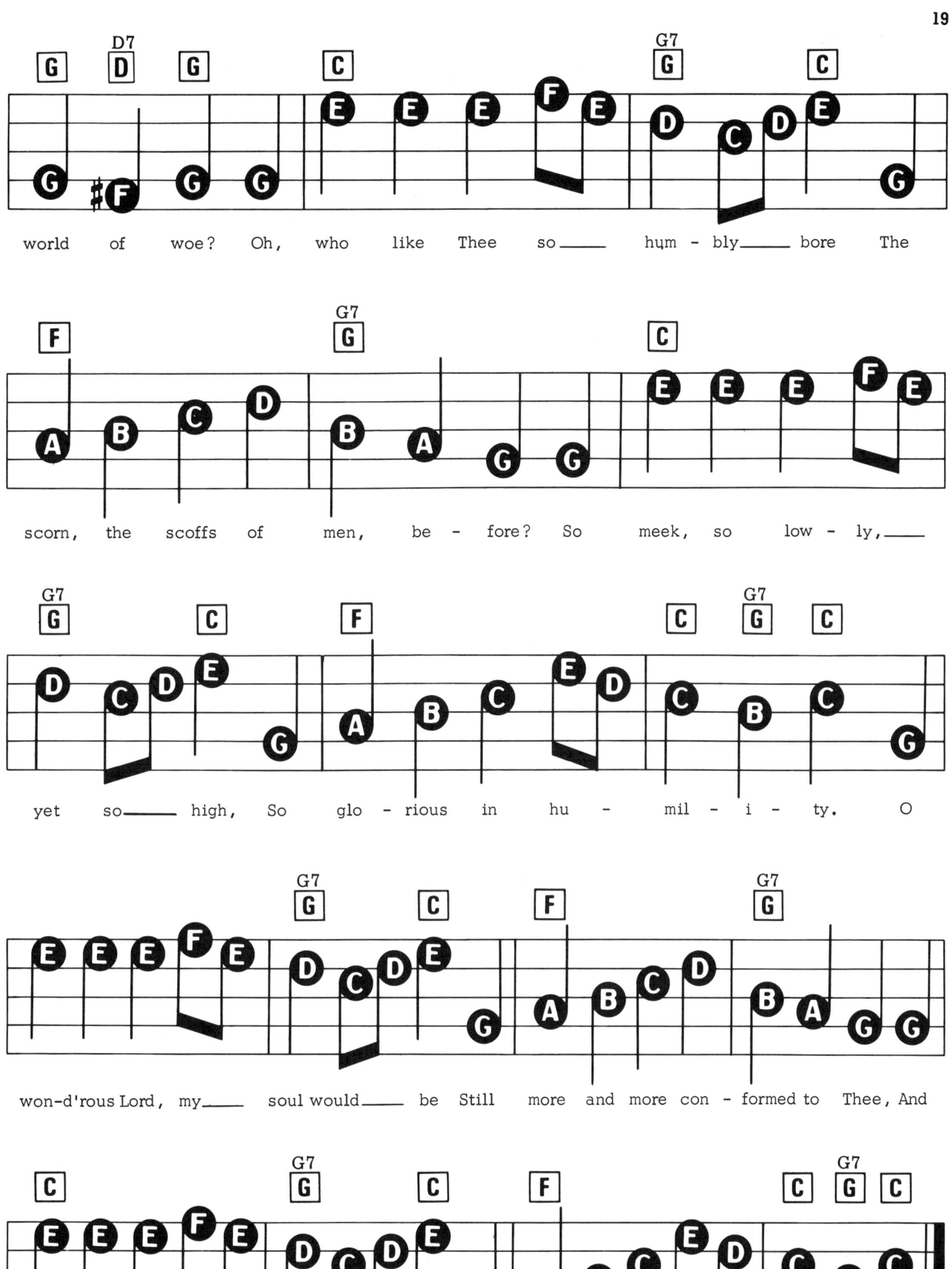

I Love To Tell The Story

Registration 4
Rhythm: March

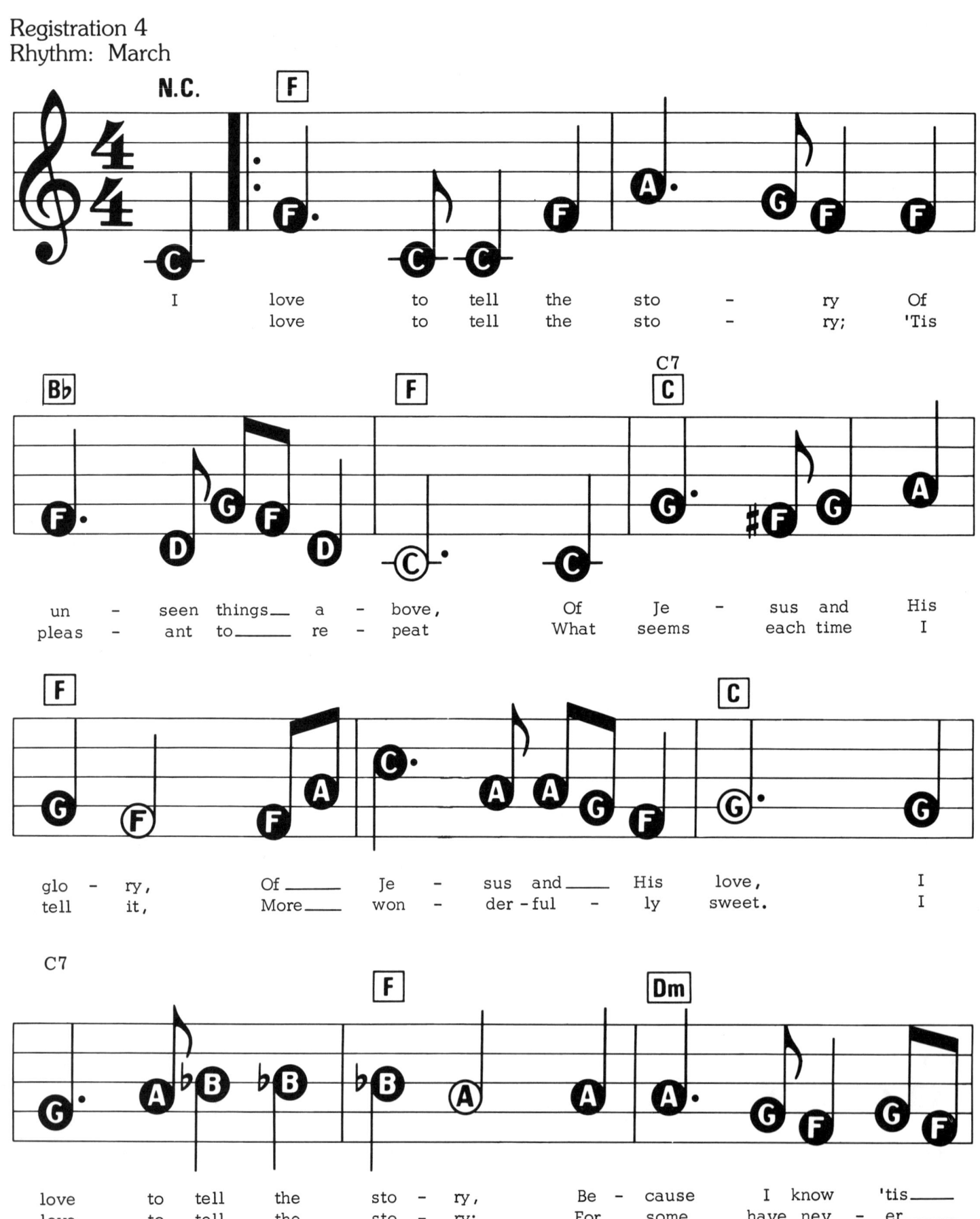

Copyright © 1991 by HAL LEONARD PUBLISHING CORPORATION
International Copyright Secured   All Rights Reserved

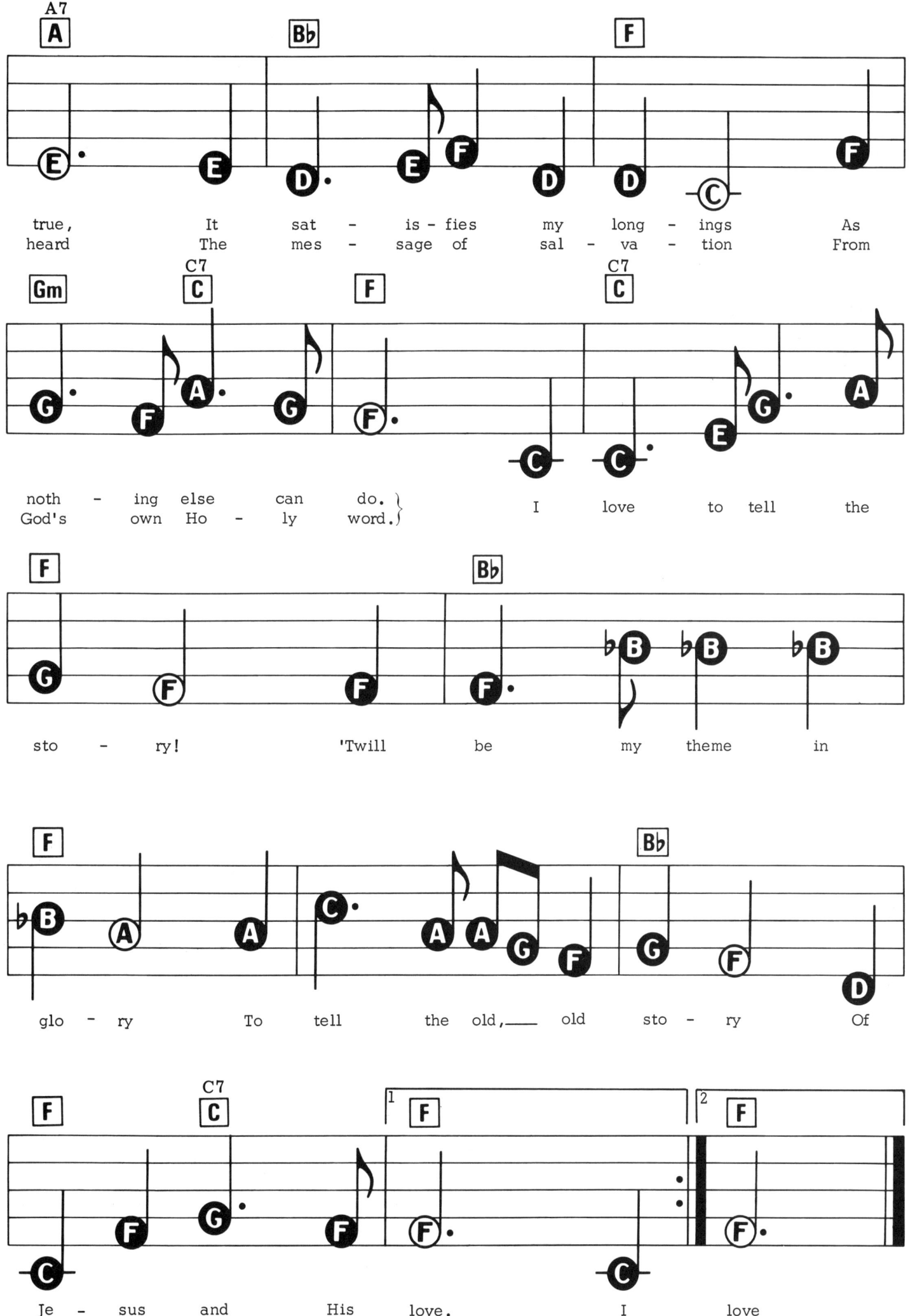

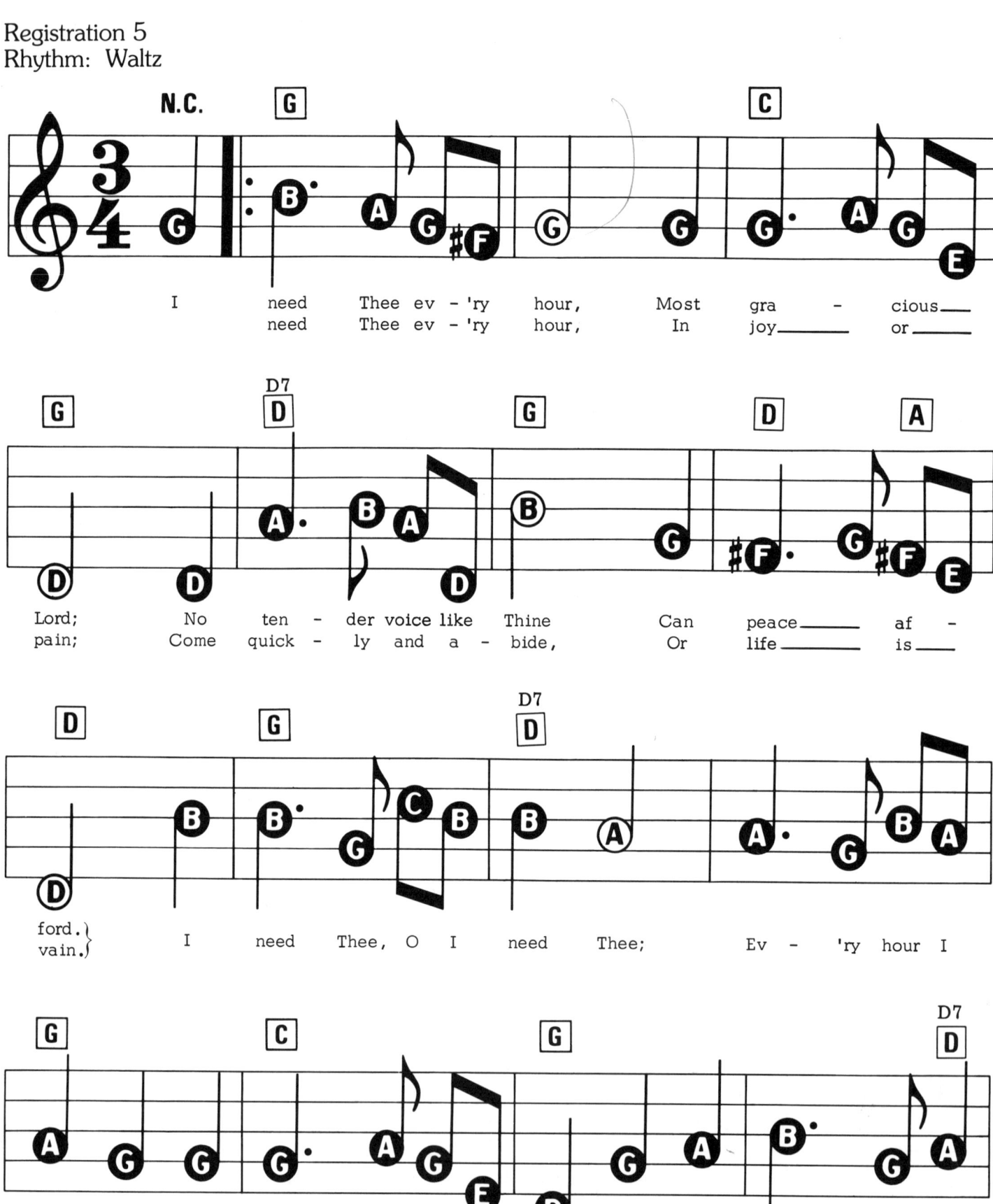

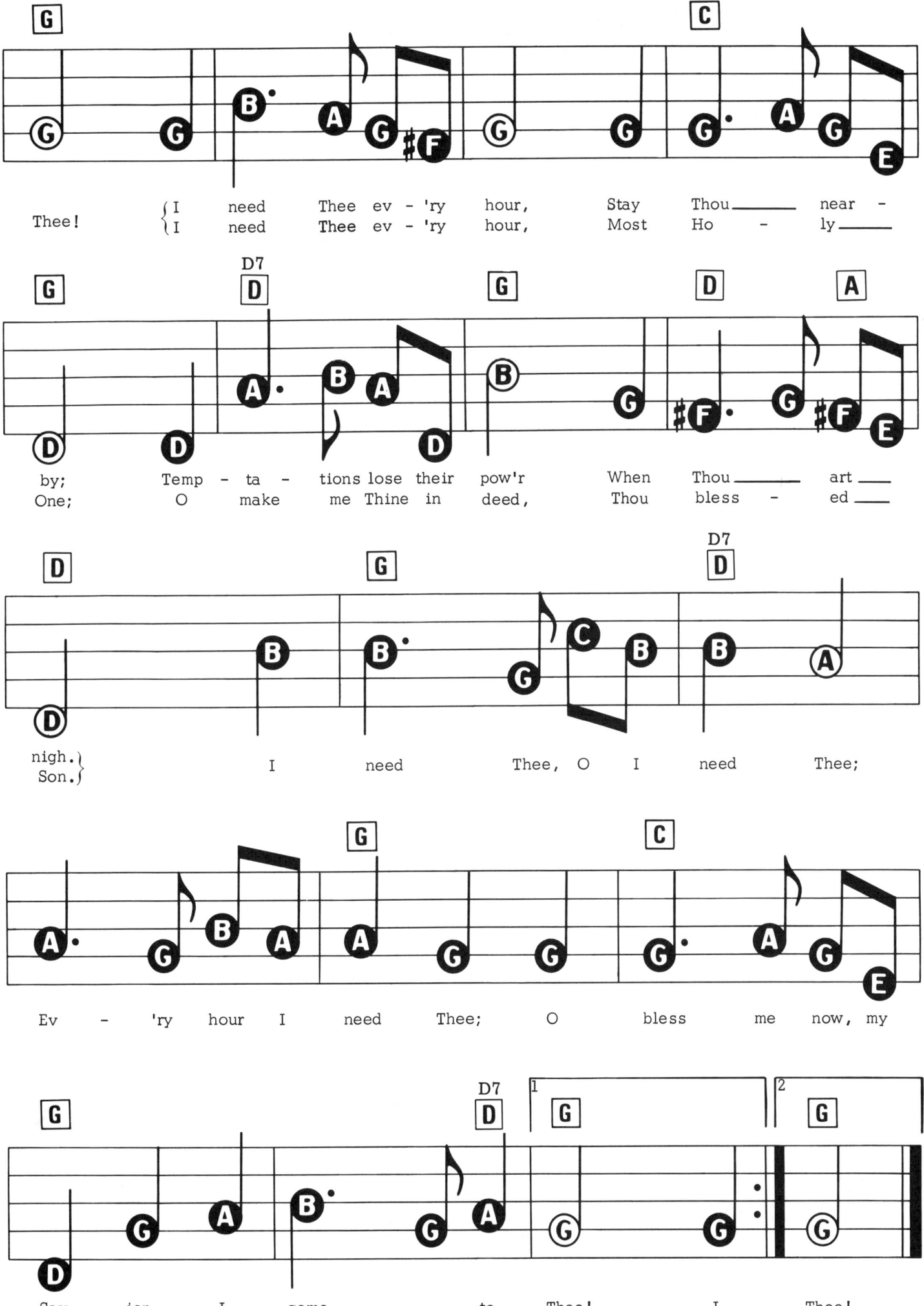

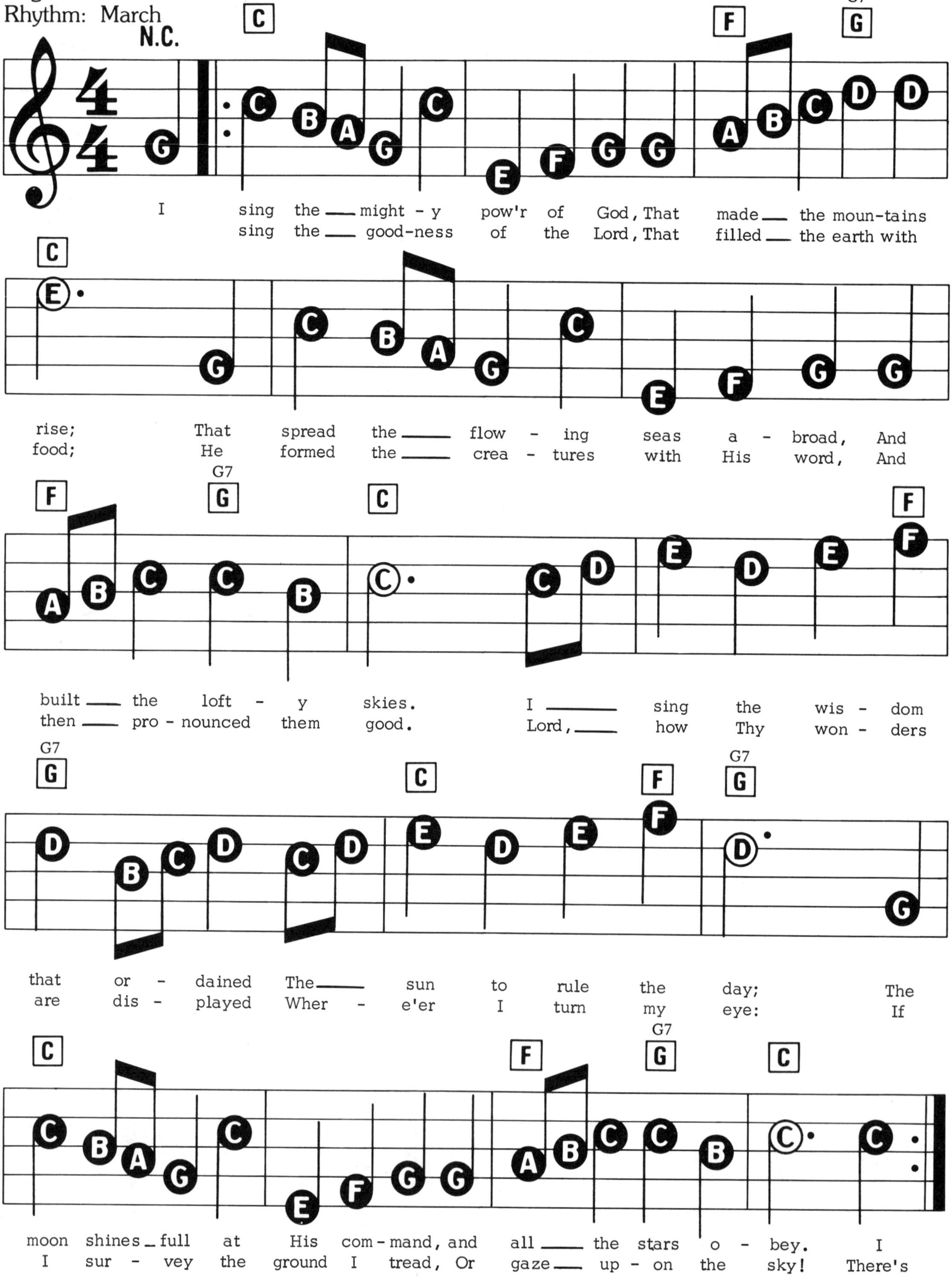

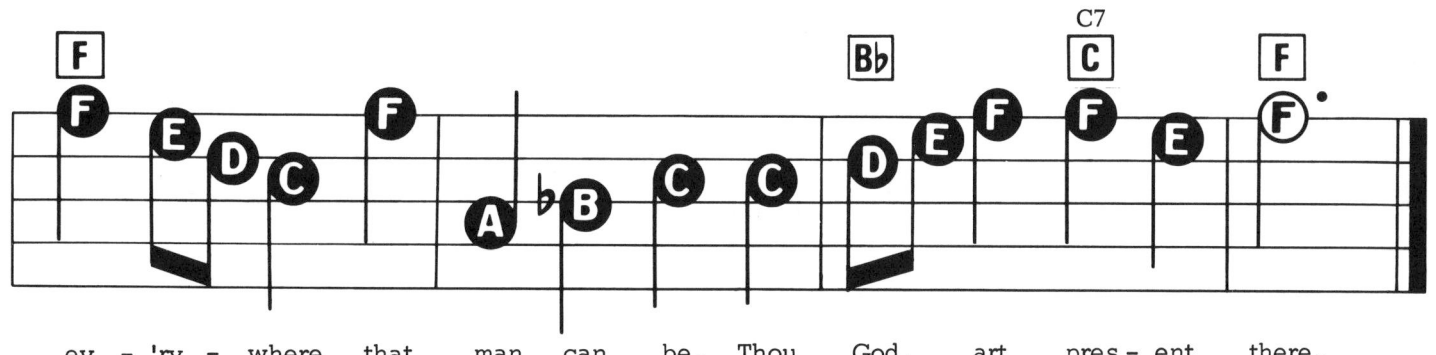

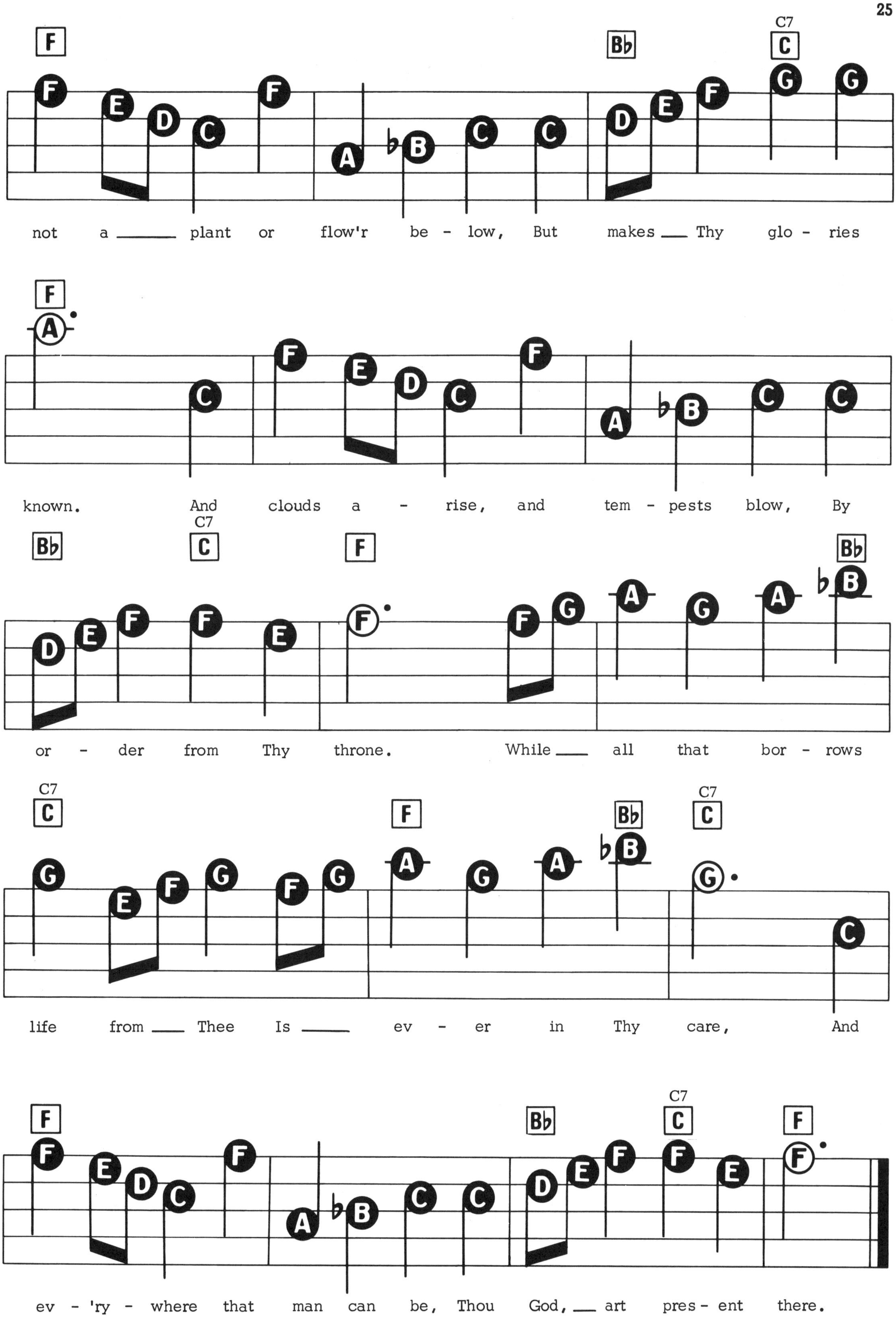

I Surrender All

Registration 2
Rhythm: Pops or 8 Beat

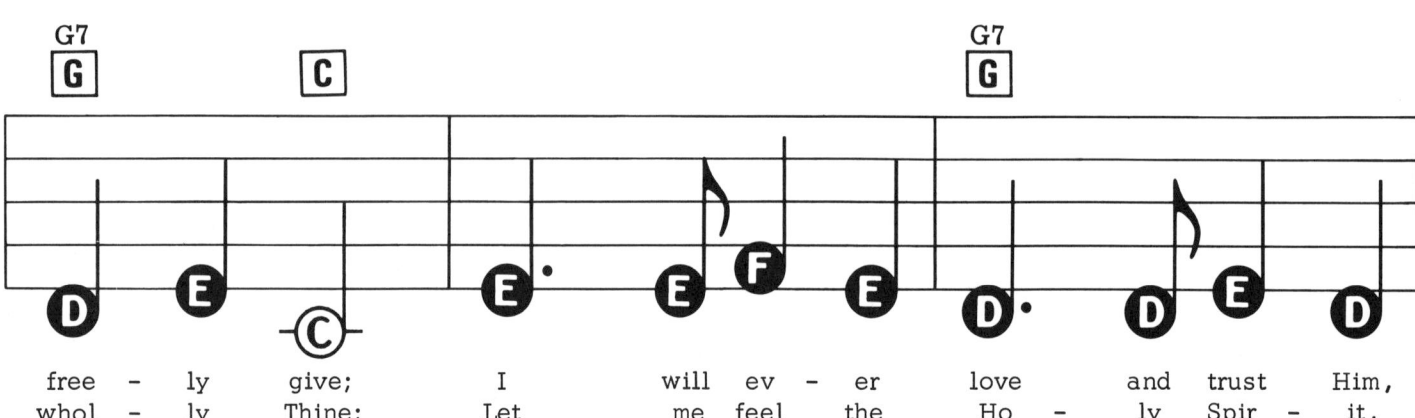

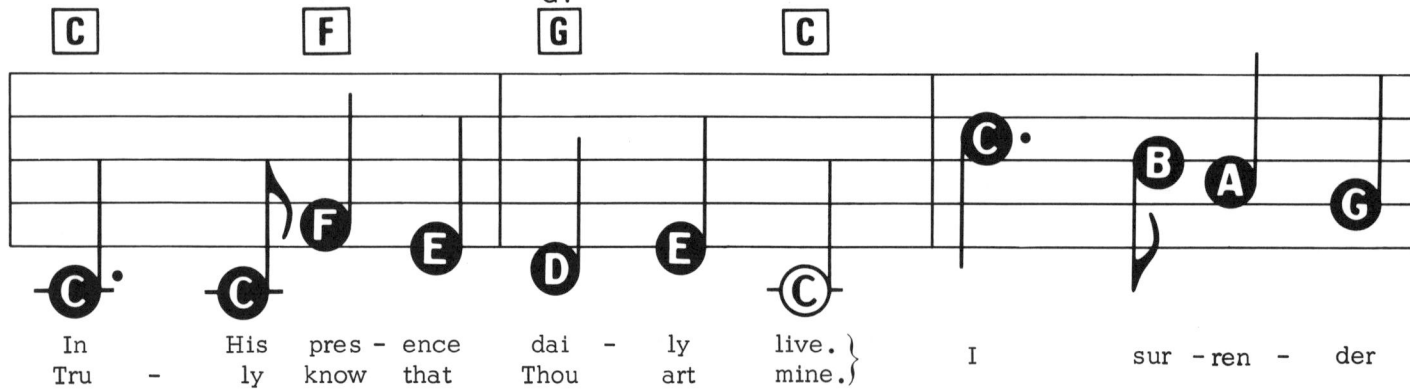

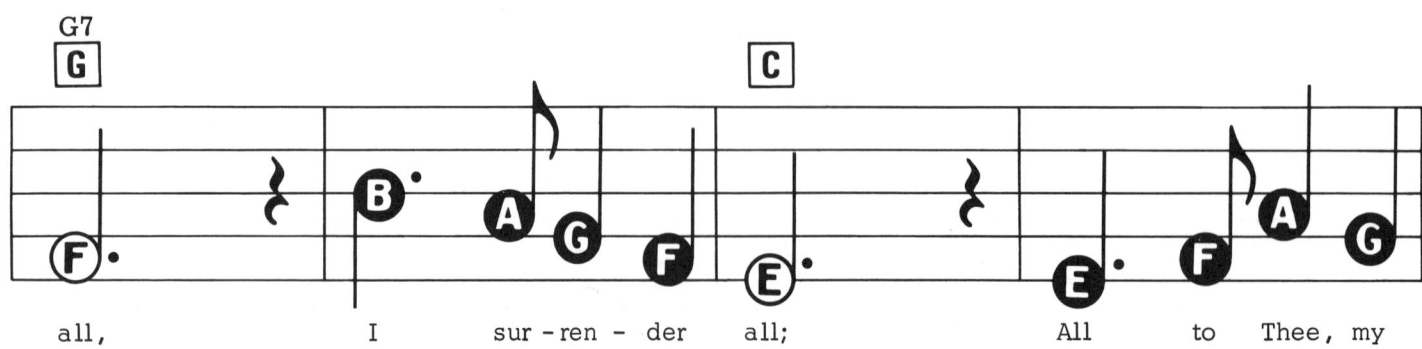

Copyright © 1991 by HAL LEONARD PUBLISHING CORPORATION
International Copyright Secured   All Rights Reserved

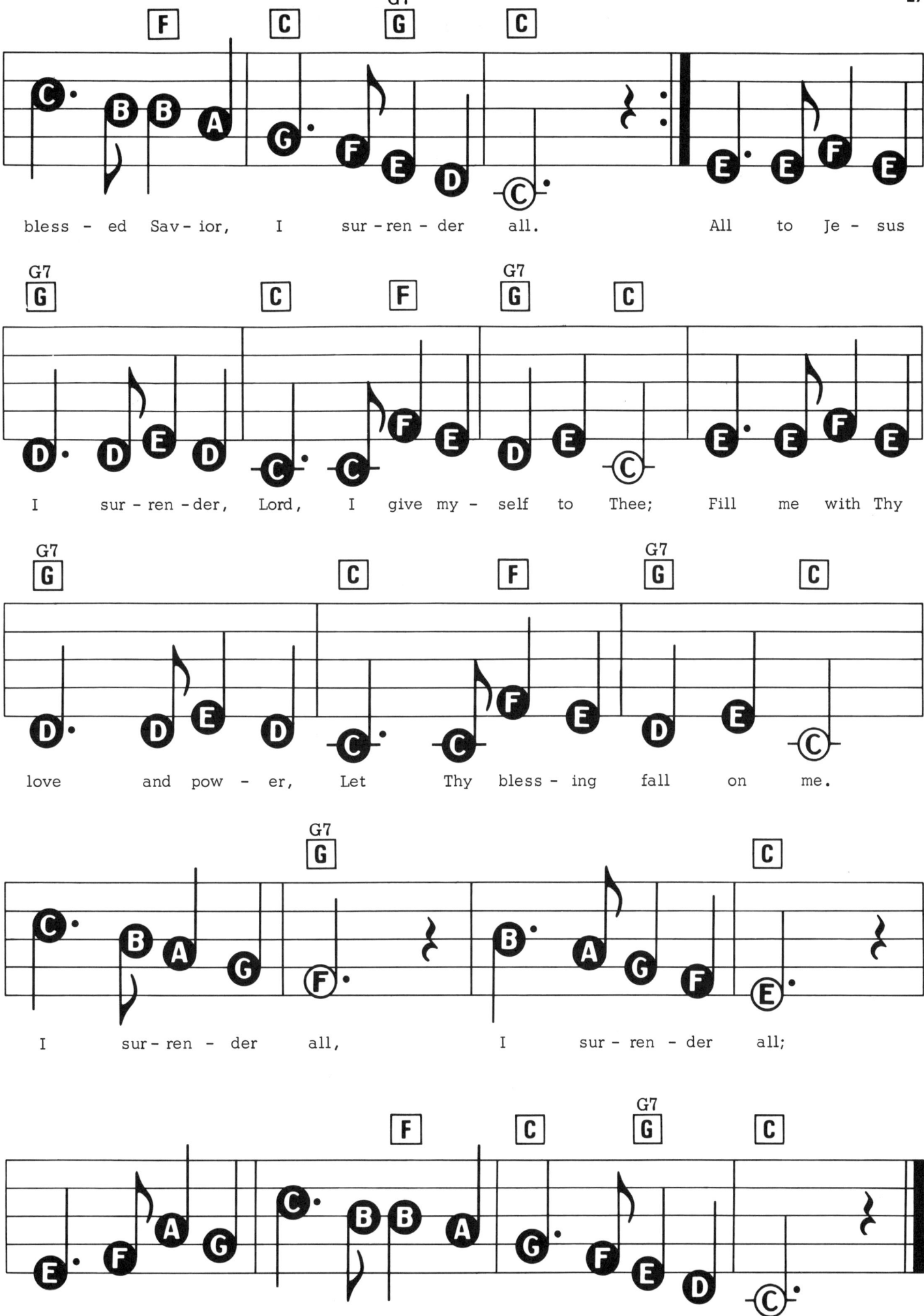

I'll Live For Him

Registration 2
Rhythm: Waltz

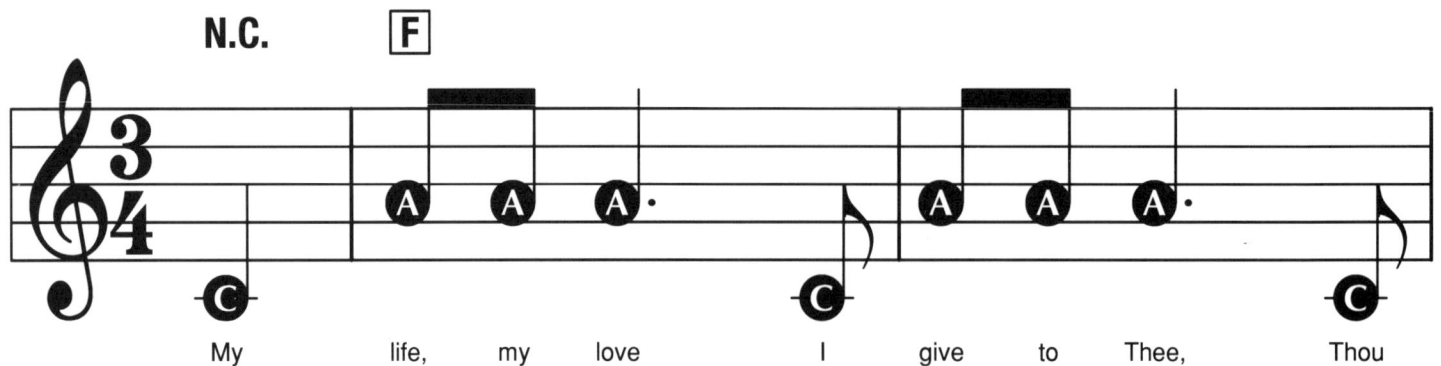
My life, my love I give to Thee, Thou

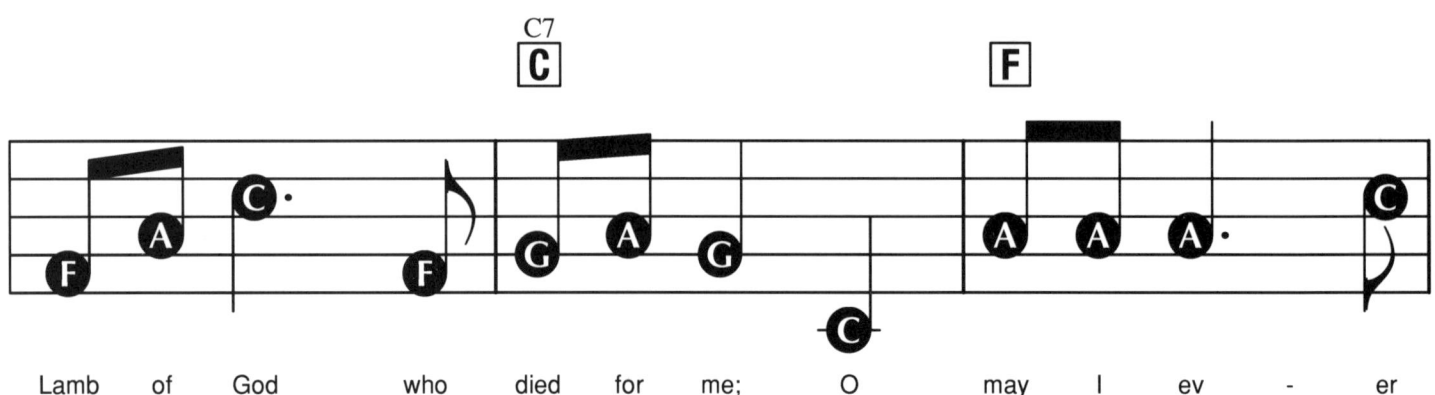
Lamb of God who died for me; O may I ev - er

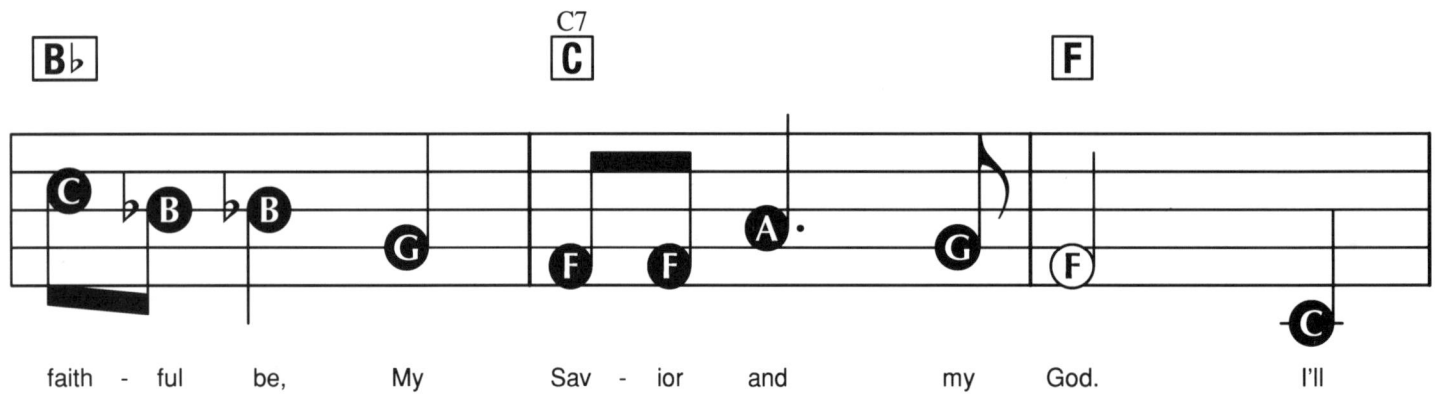
faith - ful be, My Sav - ior and my God. I'll

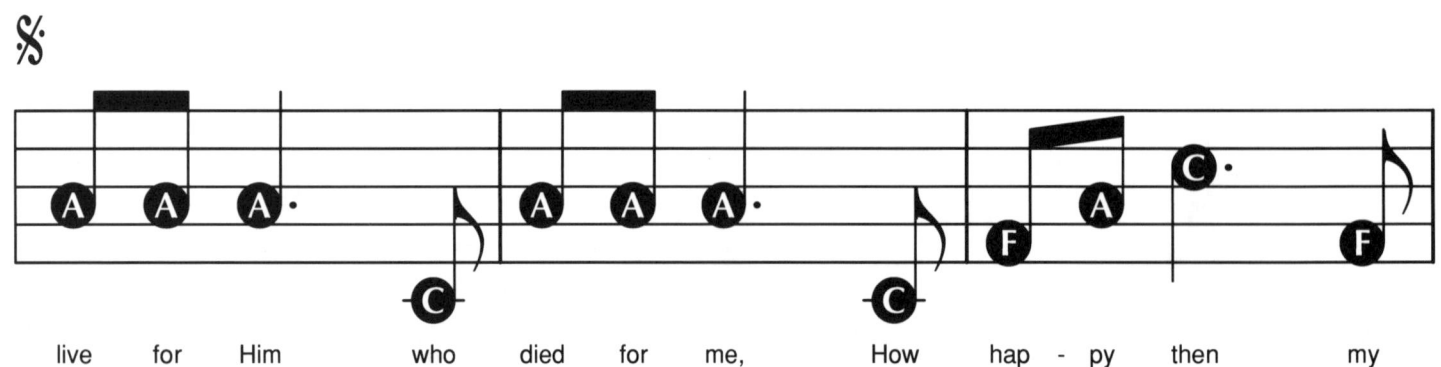
live for Him who died for me, How hap - py then my

Copyright © 1991 by HAL LEONARD PUBLISHING CORPORATION
International Copyright Secured All Rights Reserved

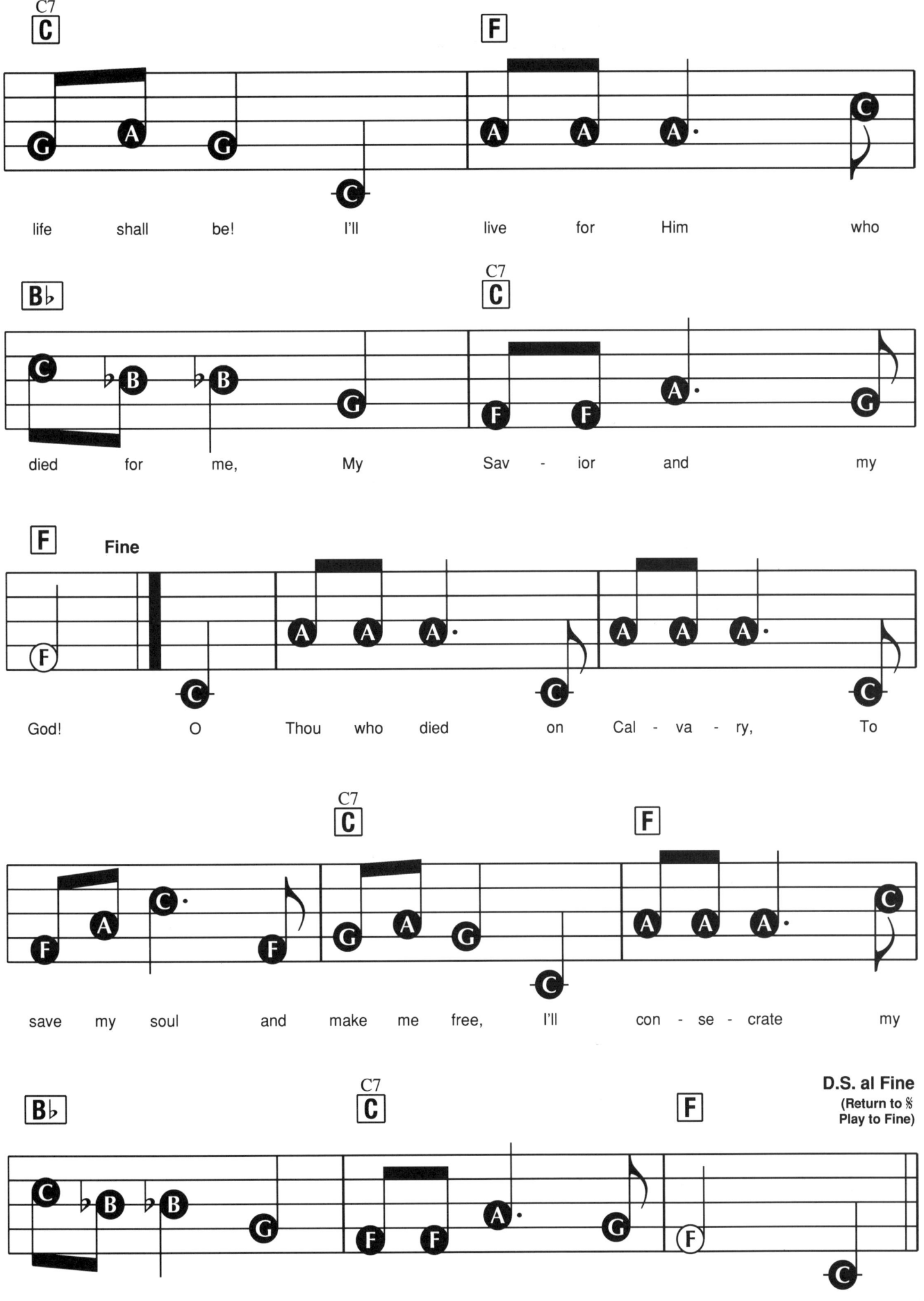

Love Lifted Me

Registration 3
Rhythm: 6/8 March or Waltz

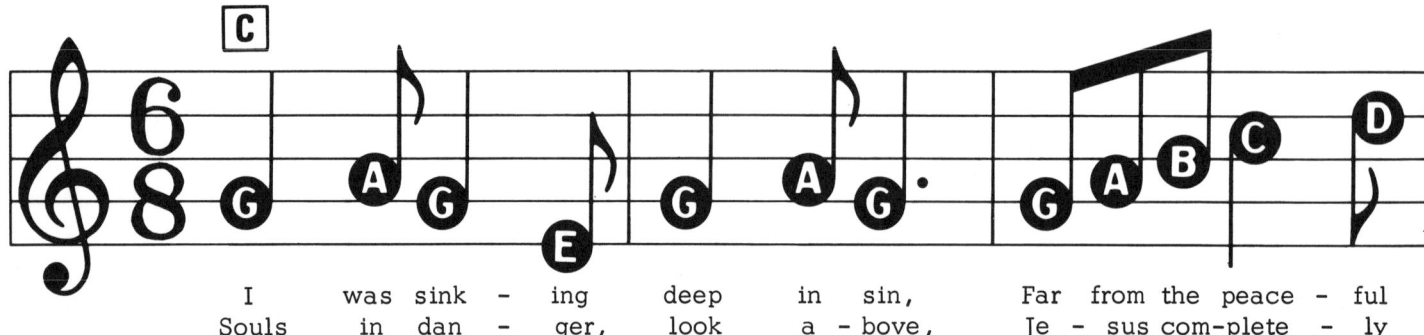

I was sink - ing deep in sin, Far from the peace - ful
Souls in dan - ger, look a - bove, Je - sus com - plete - ly

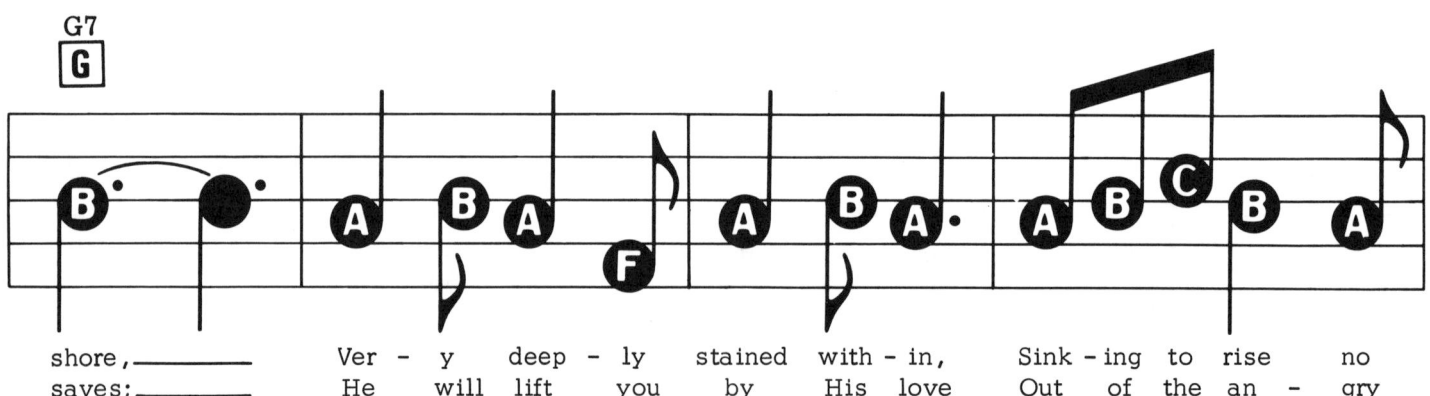

shore,_____ Ver - y deep - ly stained with - in, Sink - ing to rise no
saves;_____ He will lift you by His love Out of the an - gry

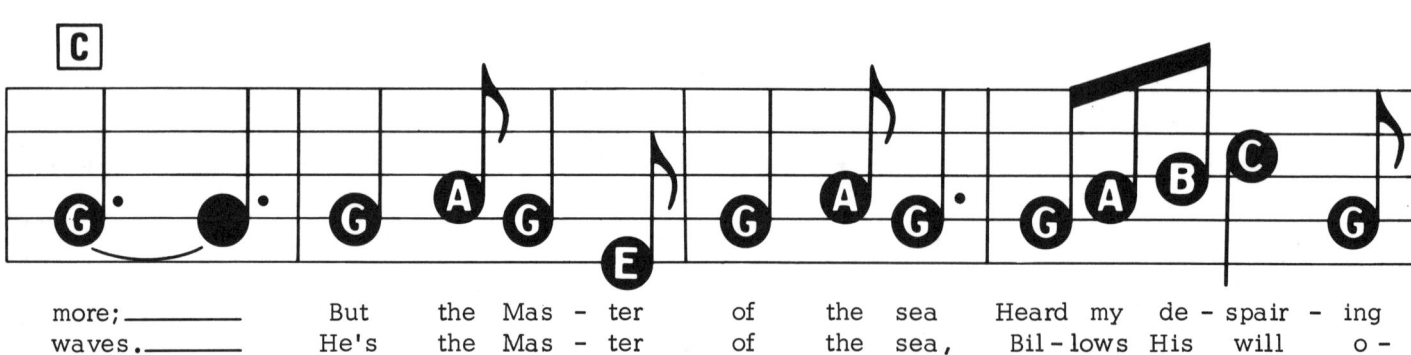

more;_____ But the Mas - ter of the sea Heard my de - spair - ing
waves._____ He's the Mas - ter of the sea, Bil - lows His will o -

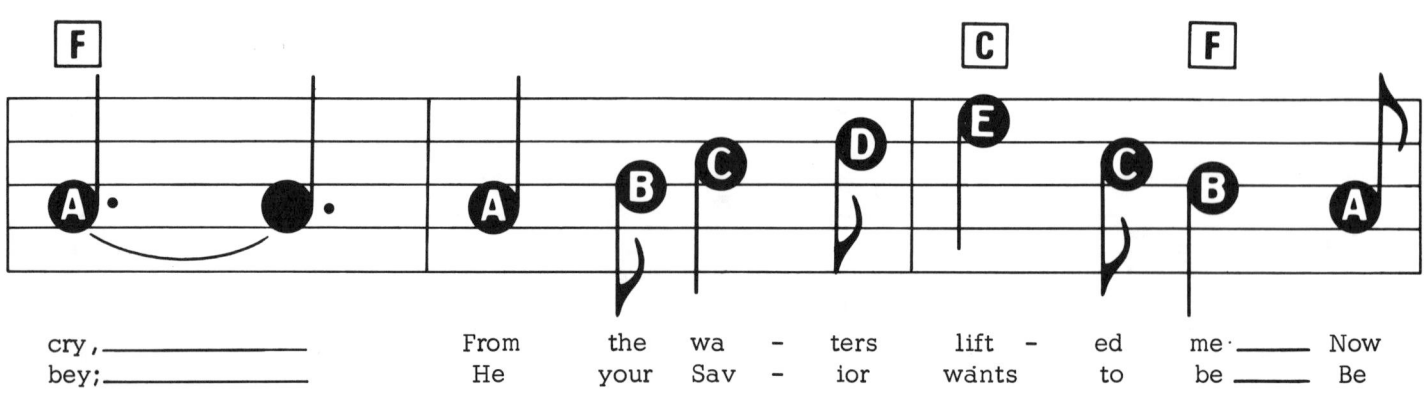

cry,_____ From the wa - ters lift - ed me._____ Now
bey;_____ He your Sav - ior wants to be_____ Be

Copyright © 1991 by HAL LEONARD PUBLISHING CORPORATION
International Copyright Secured   All Rights Reserved

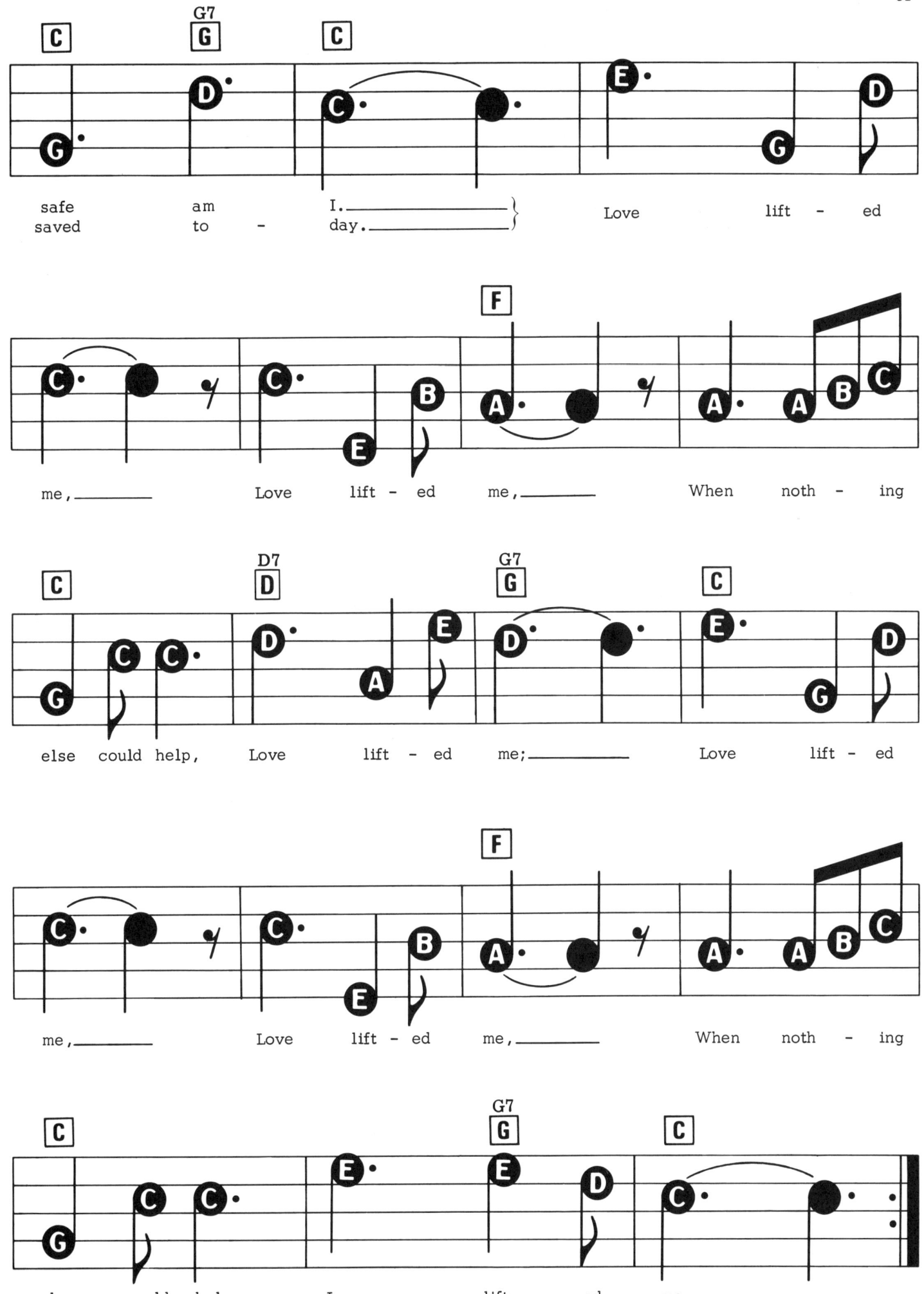

Nearer, My God, To Thee

Registration 2
Rhythm: 8 Beat or Pops

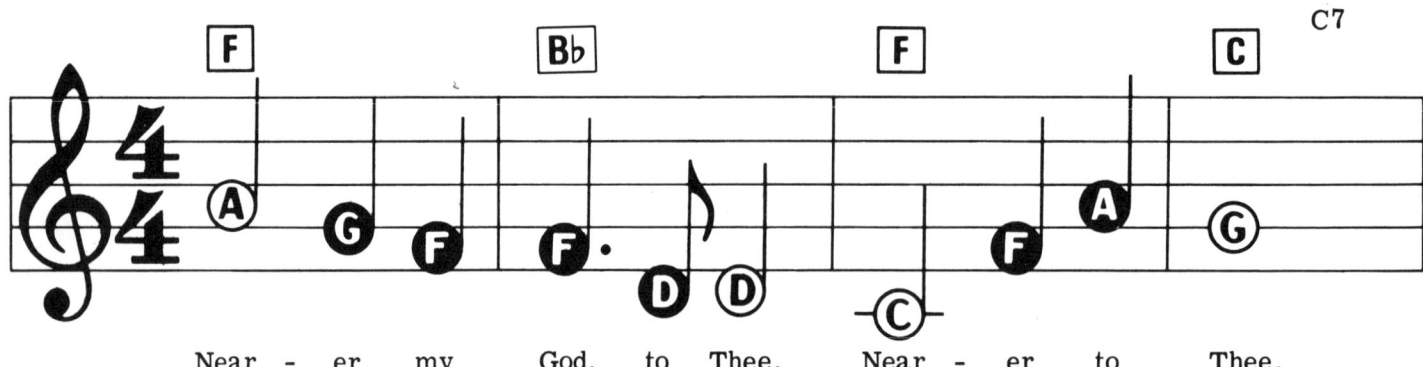

Near - er, my God, to Thee, Near - er to Thee,

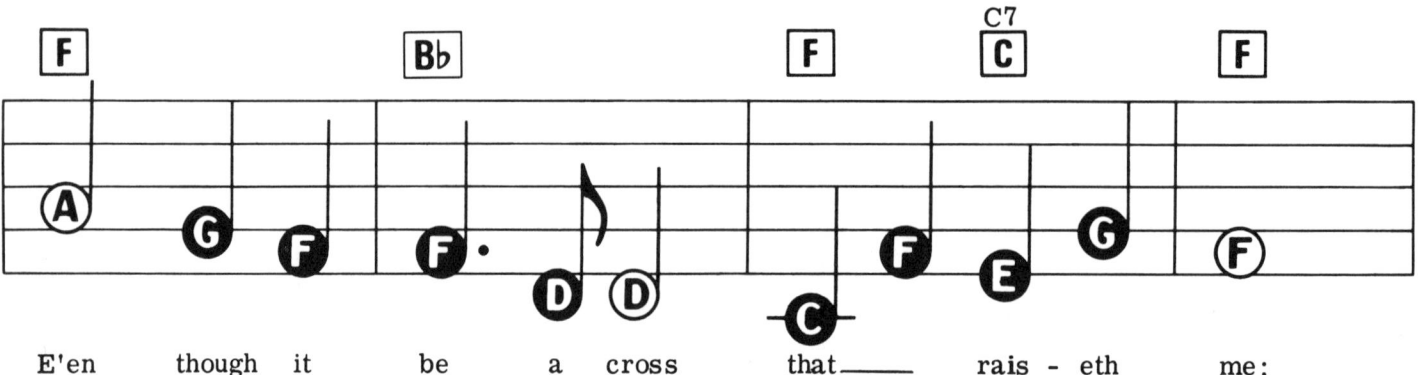

E'en though it be a cross that ___ rais - eth me;

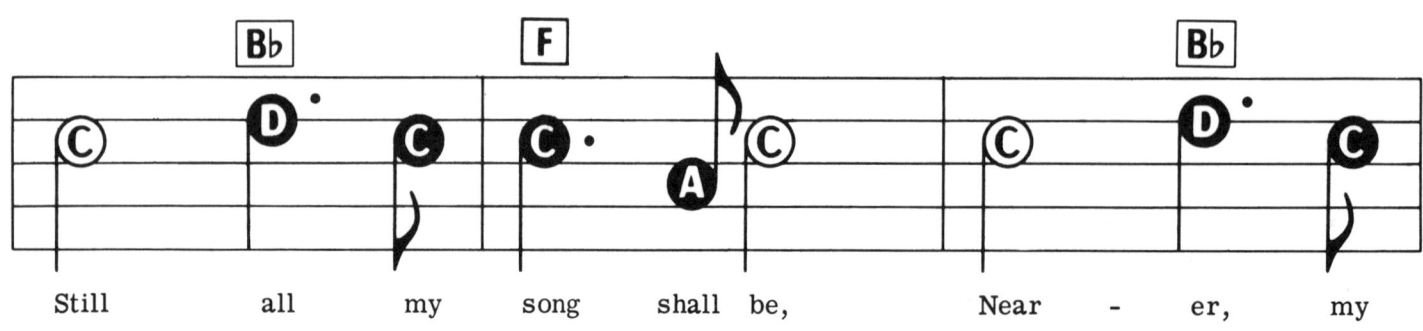

Still all my song shall be, Near - er, my

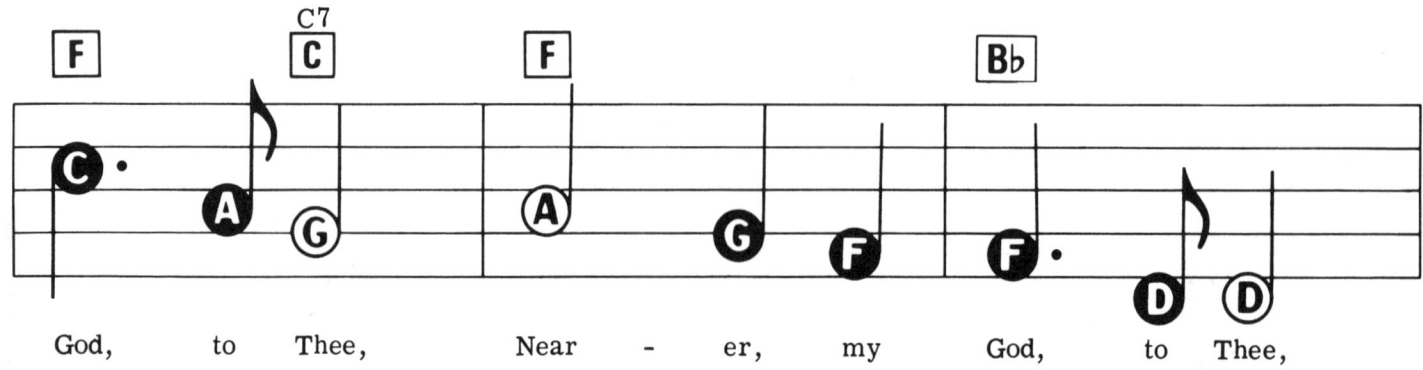

God, to Thee, Near - er, my God, to Thee,

Copyright © 1991 by HAL LEONARD PUBLISHING CORPORATION
International Copyright Secured   All Rights Reserved

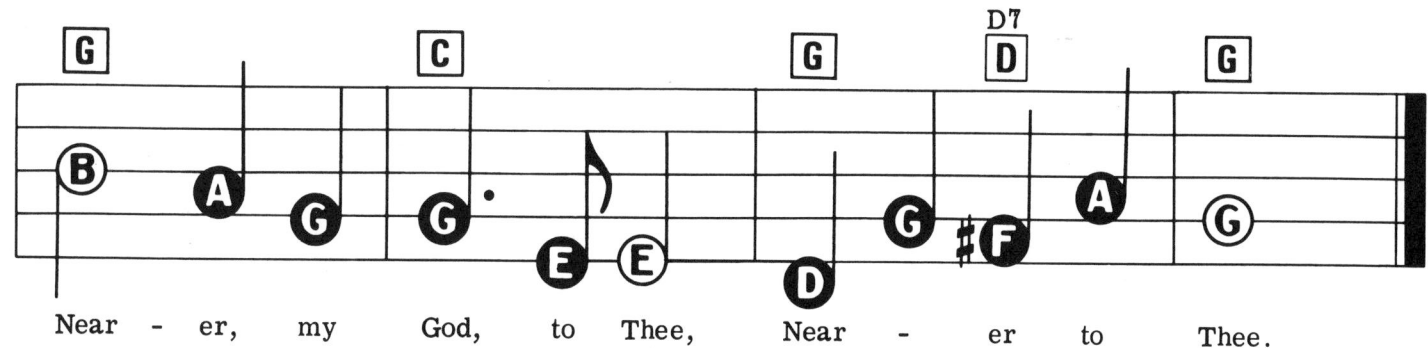

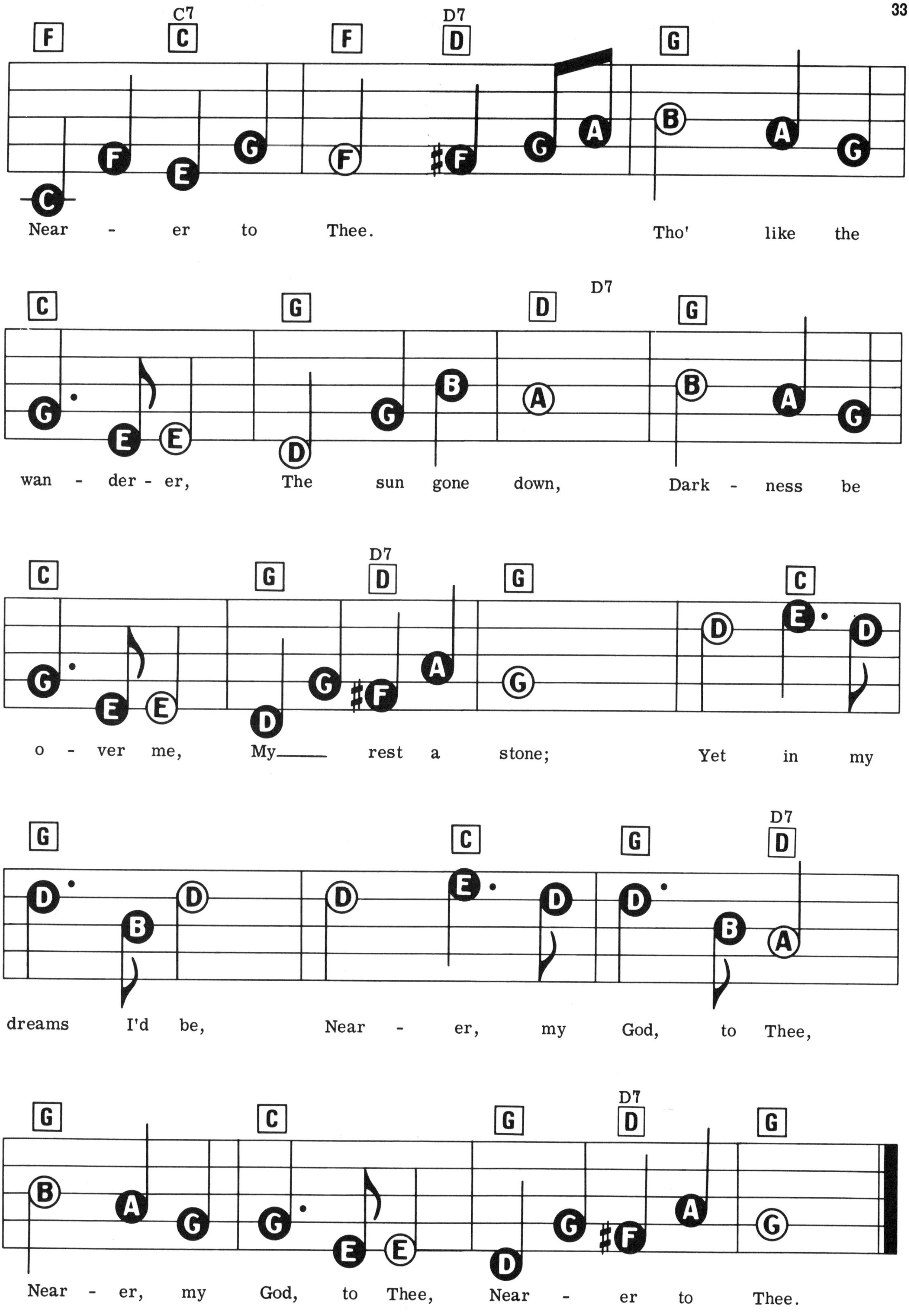

Oh, How I Love Jesus

Registration 2
Rhythm: 6/8 March or Waltz

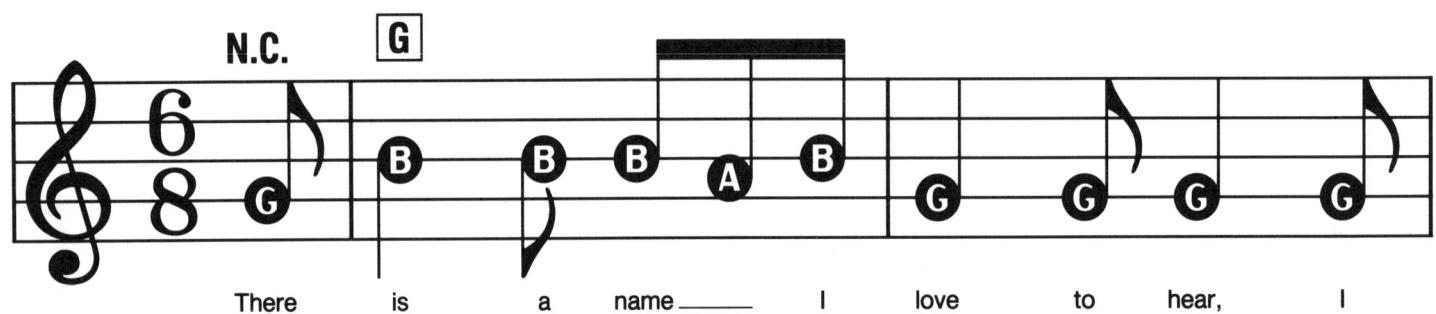

There is a name ___ I love to hear, I

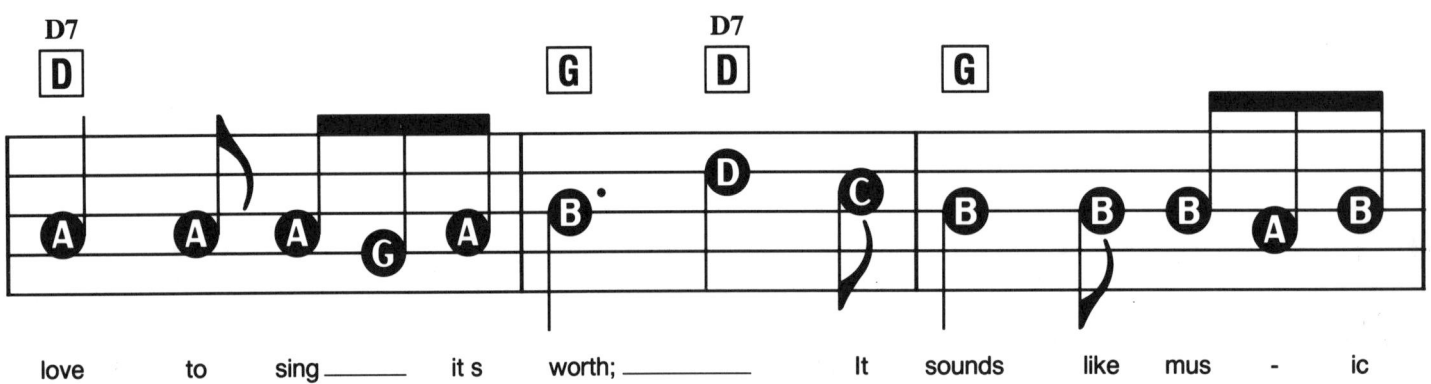

love to sing ___ it's worth; ___ It sounds like mus - ic

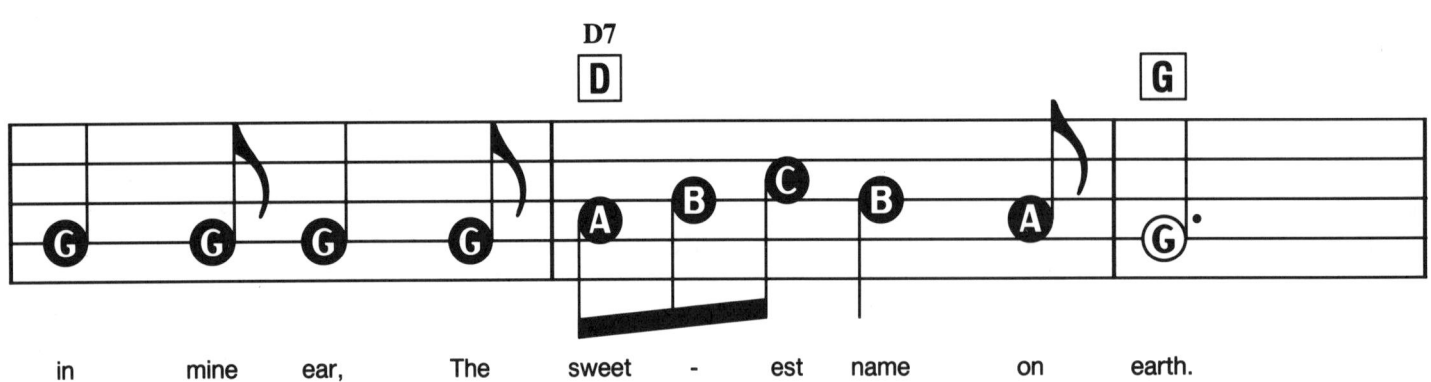

in mine ear, The sweet - est name on earth.

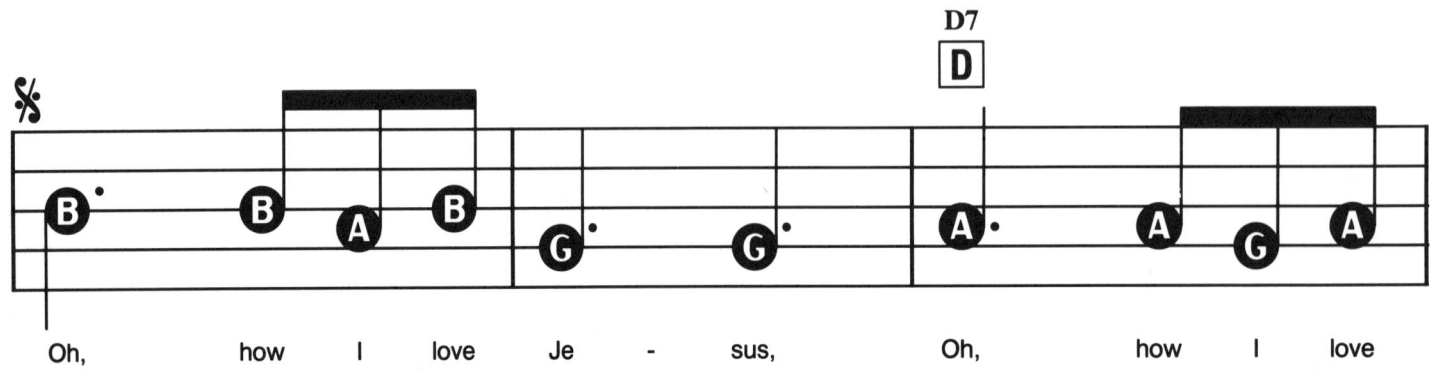

Oh, how I love Je - sus, Oh, how I love

Copyright © 1991 by HAL LEONARD PUBLISHING CORPORATION
International Copyright Secured   All Rights Reserved

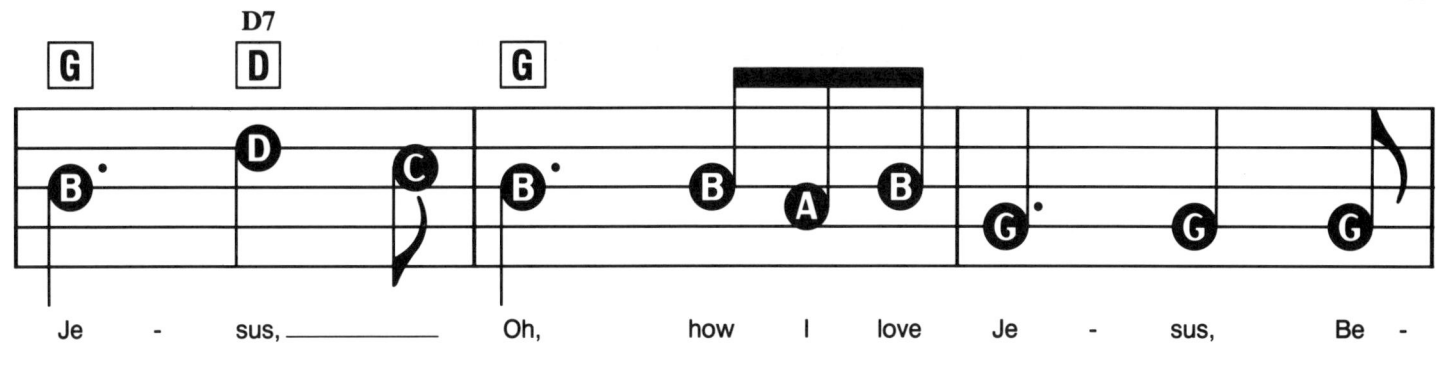
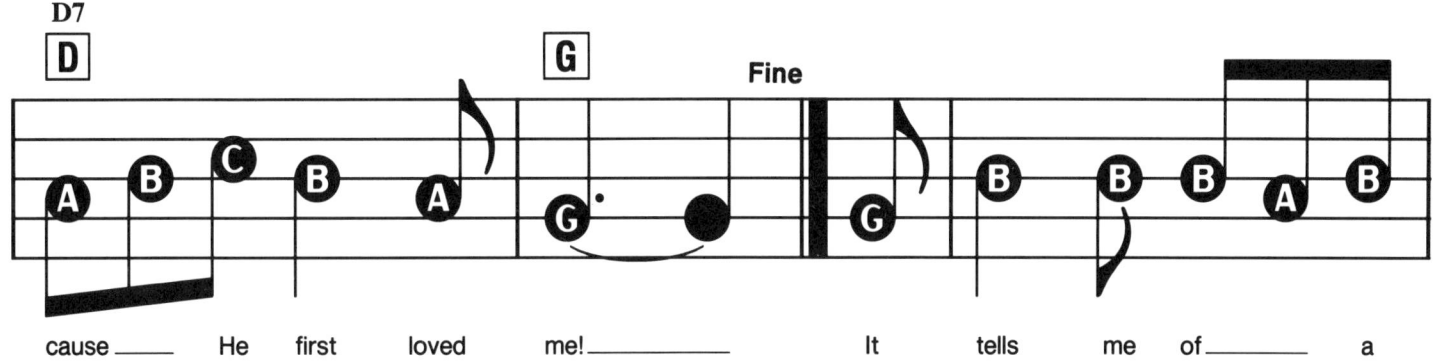
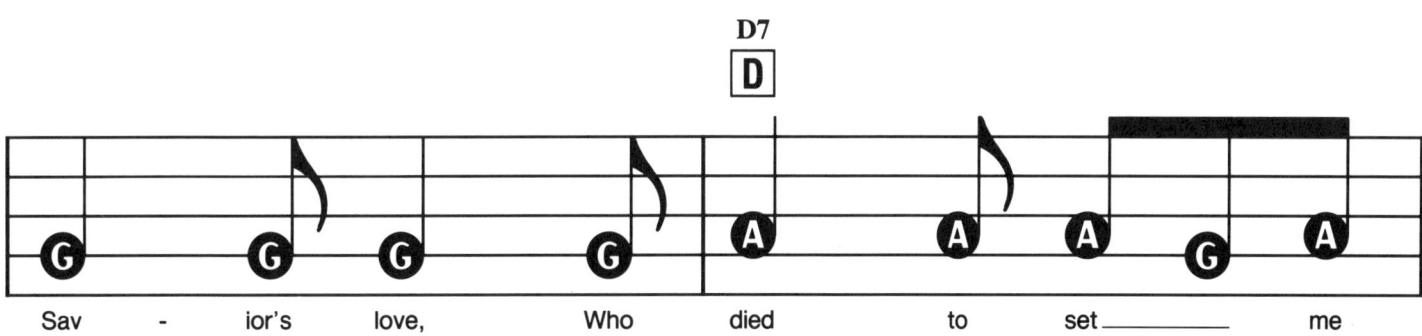
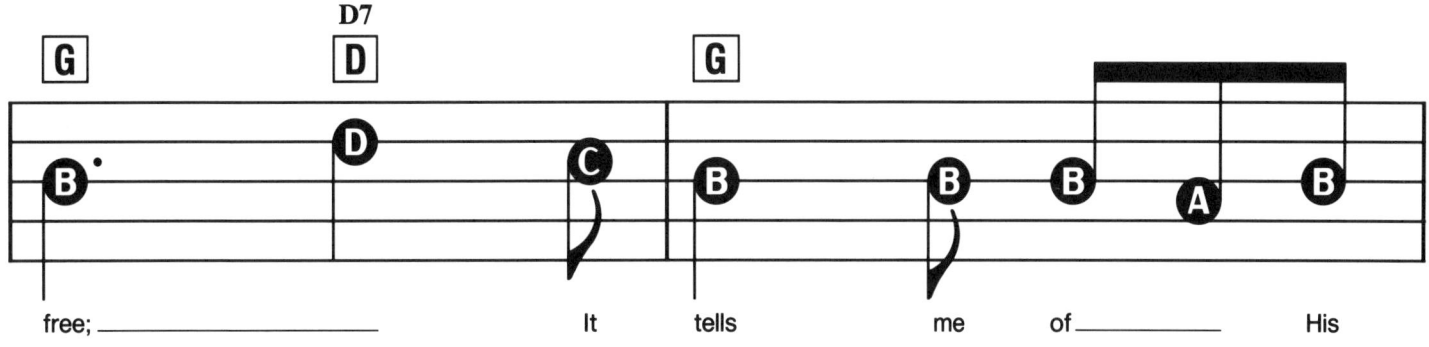
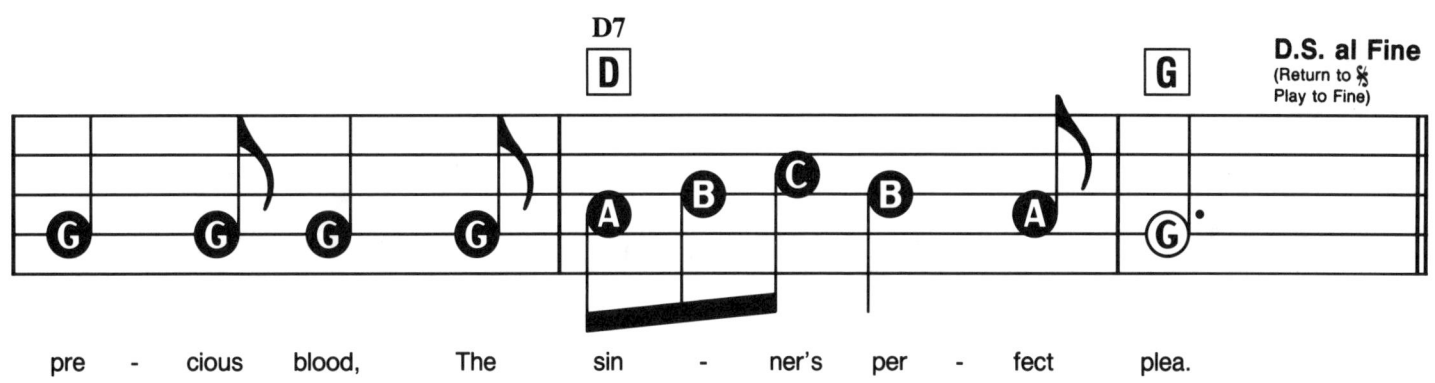

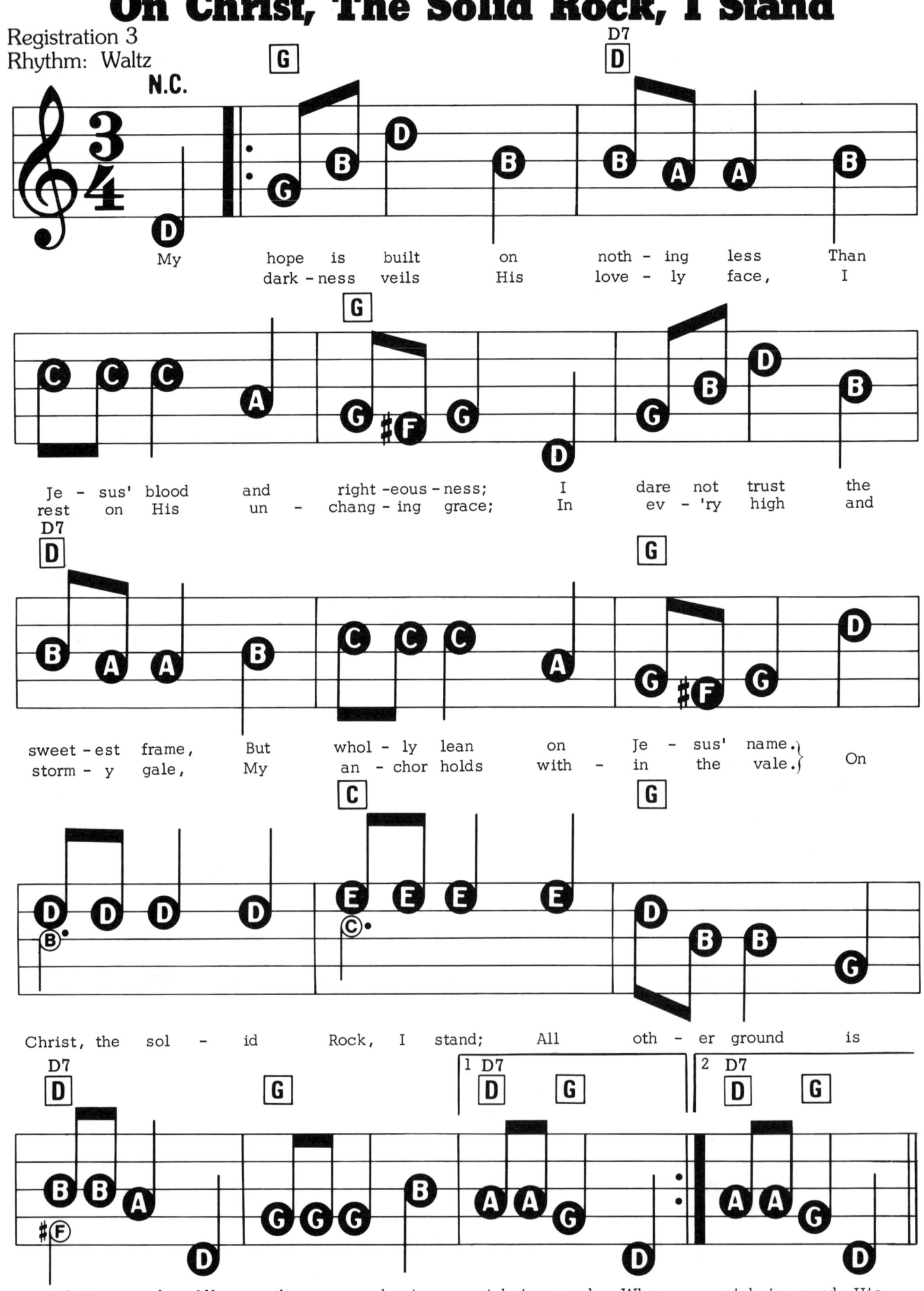

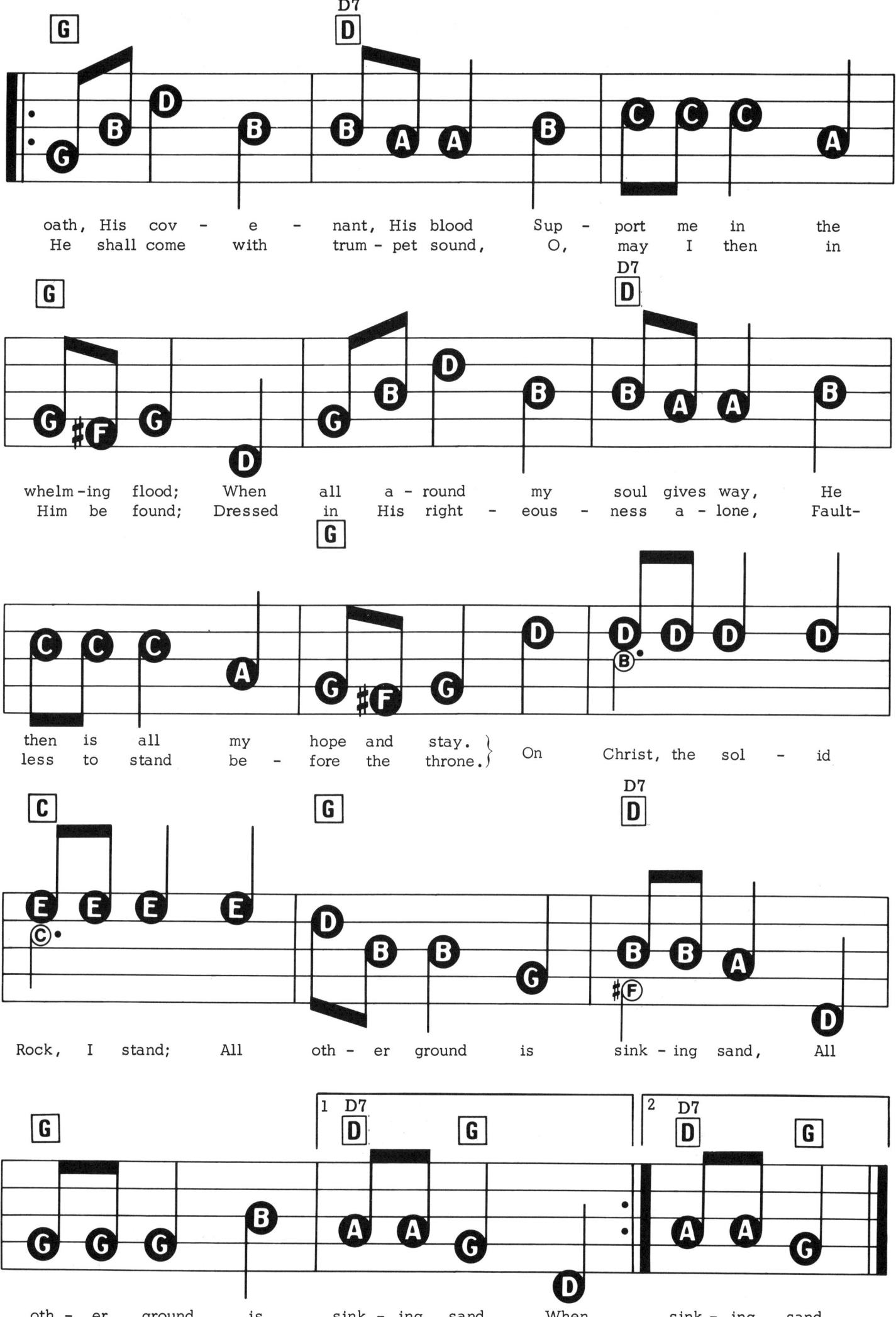

Have You Any Room For Jesus?

Registration 6
Rhythm: Swing

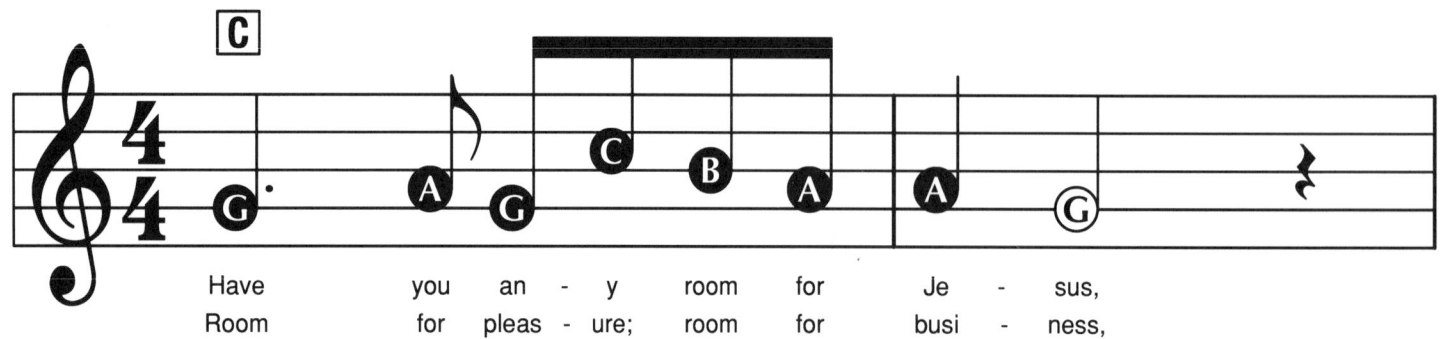
Have you an-y room for Je - sus,
Room for pleas - ure; room for busi - ness,

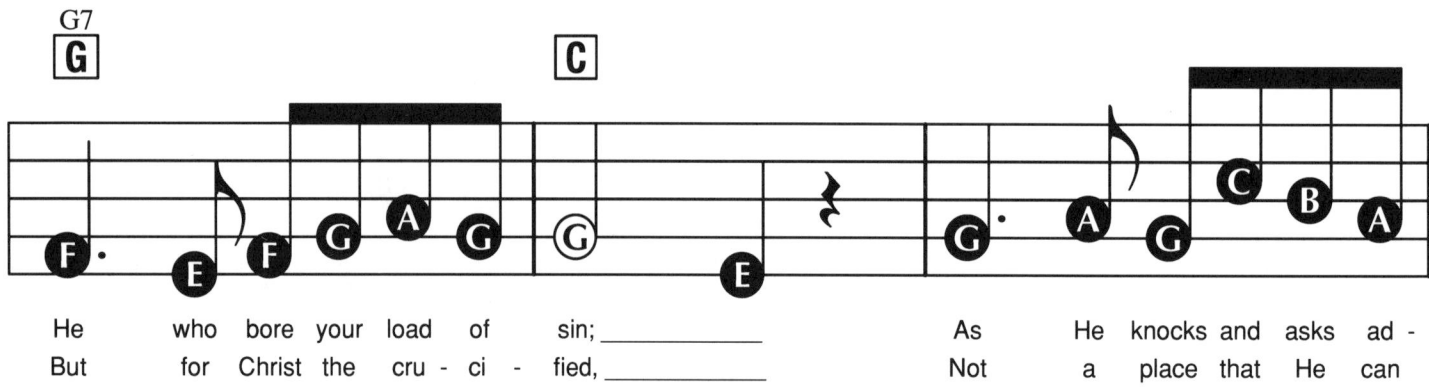
He who bore your load of sin; As He knocks and asks ad -
But for Christ the cru - ci - fied, Not a place that He can

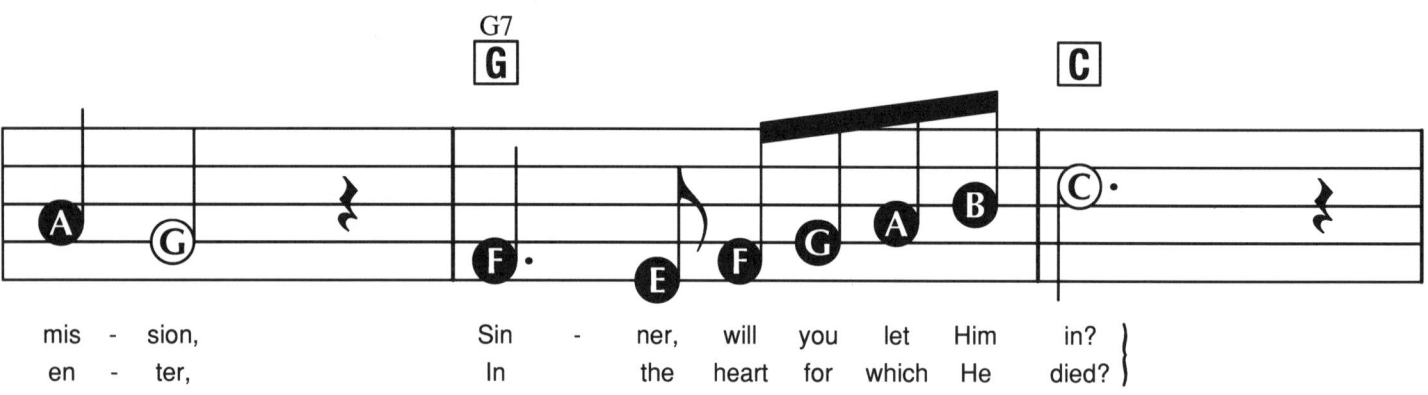
mis - sion, Sin - ner, will you let Him in?
en - ter, In the heart for which He died?

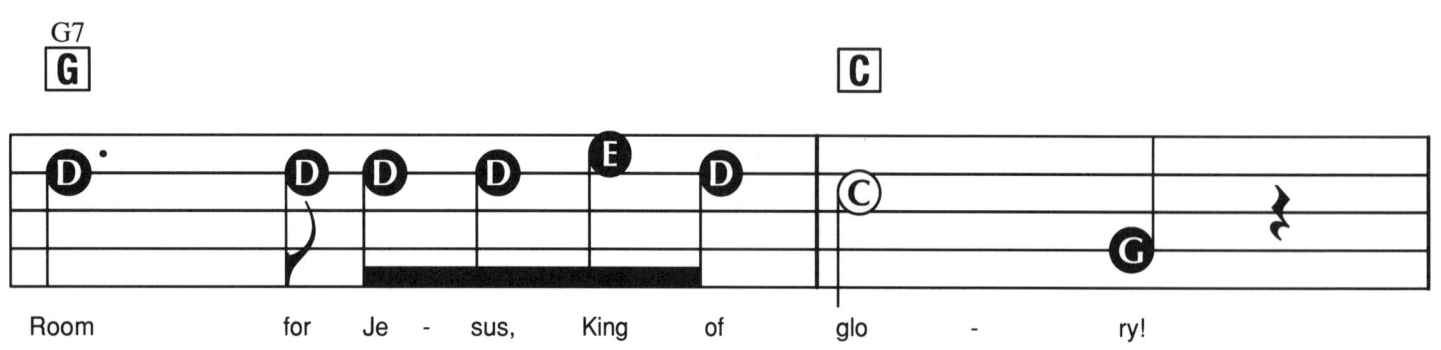
Room for Je - sus, King of glo - ry!

Copyright © 1991 by HAL LEONARD PUBLISHING CORPORATION
International Copyright Secured   All Rights Reserved

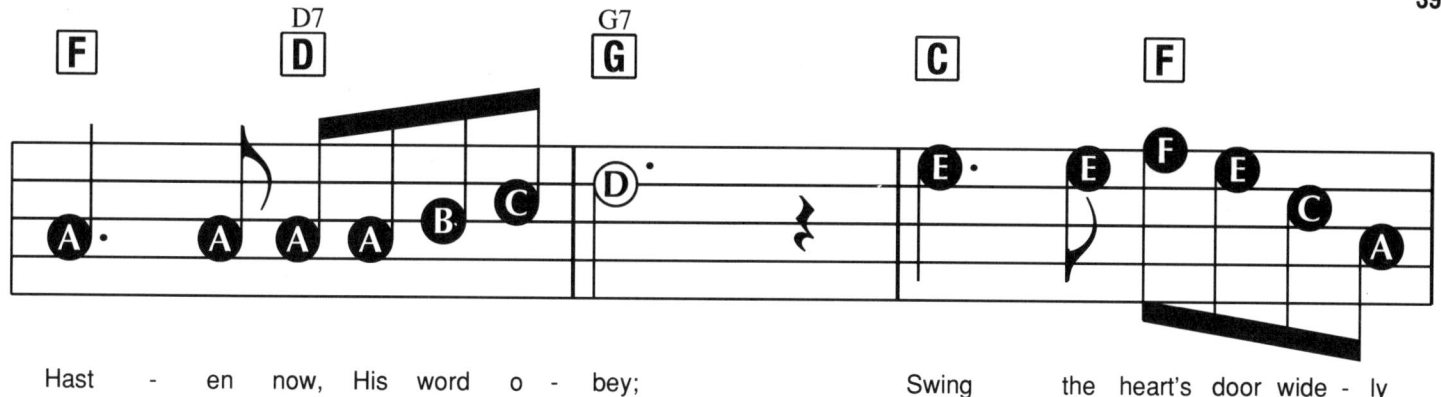
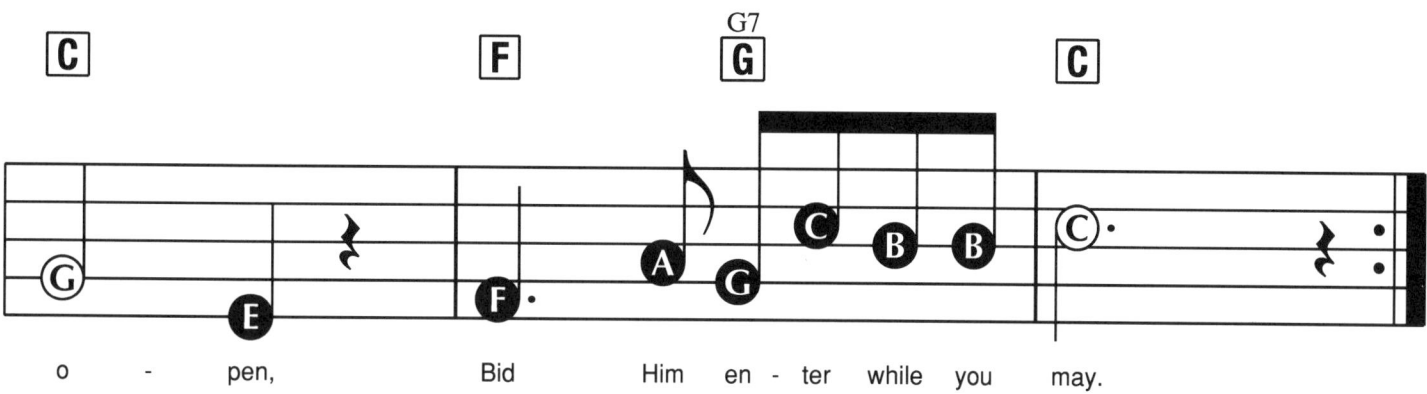
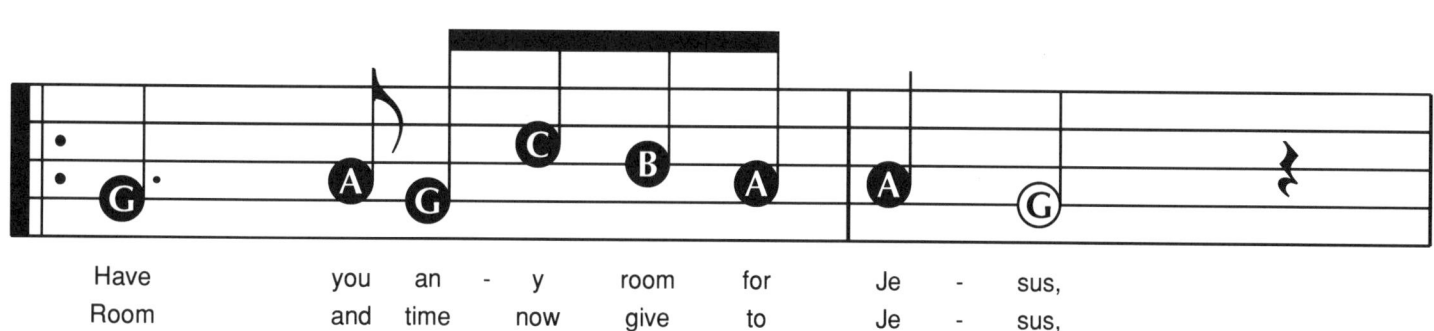
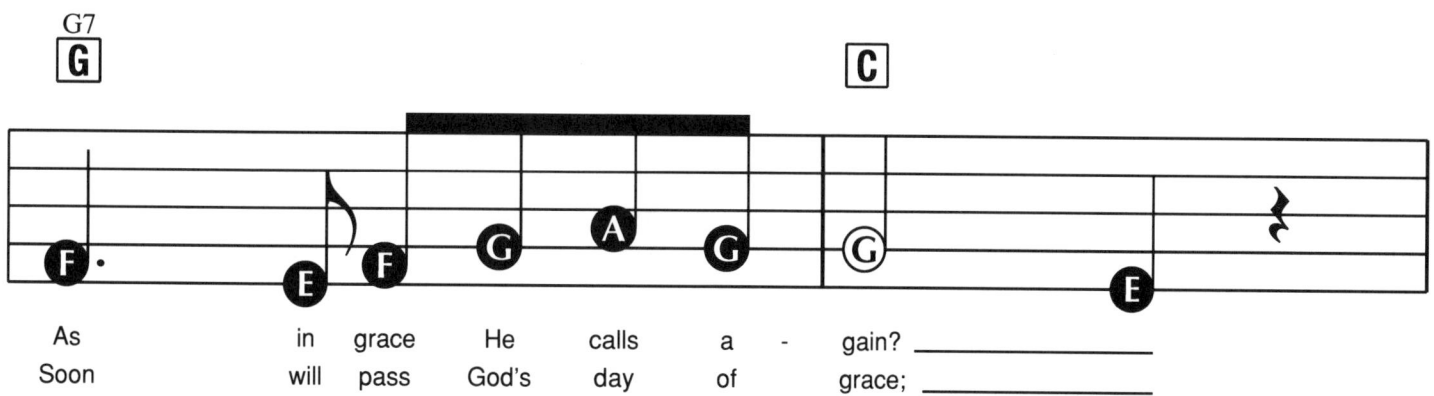

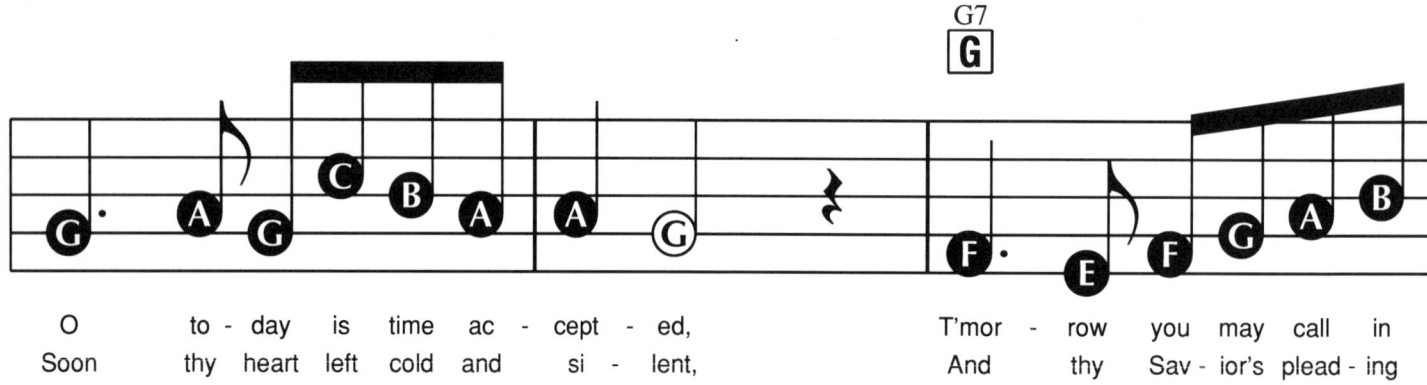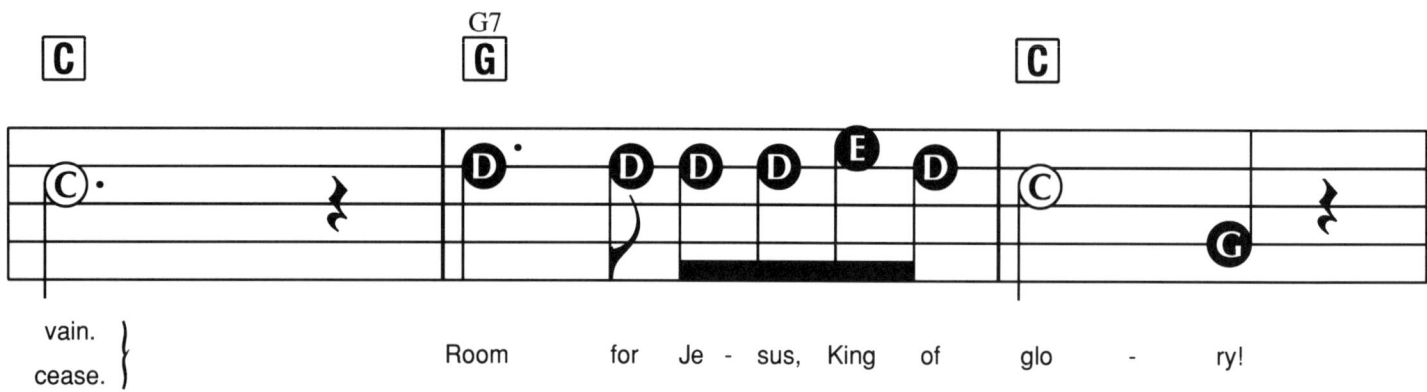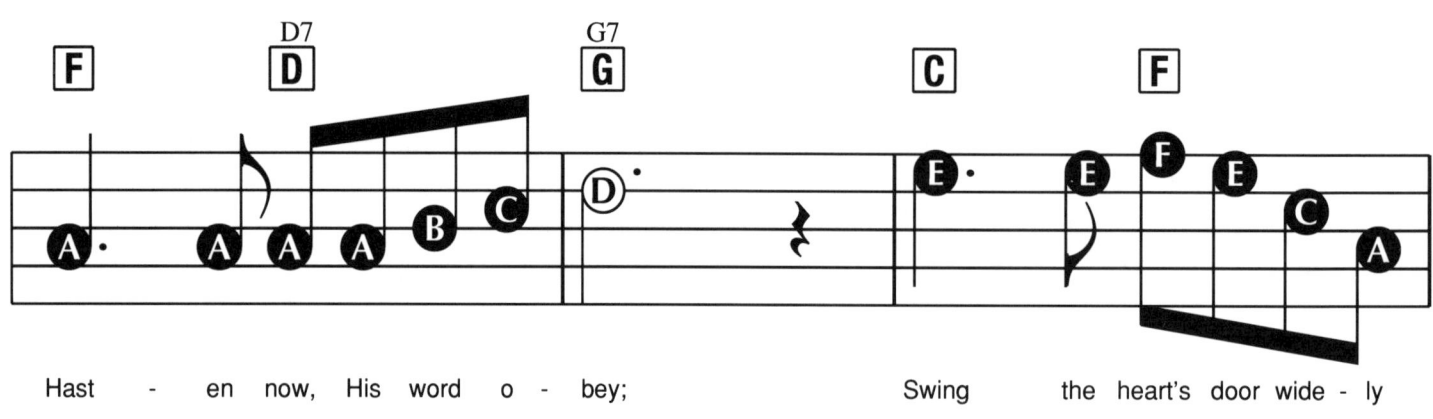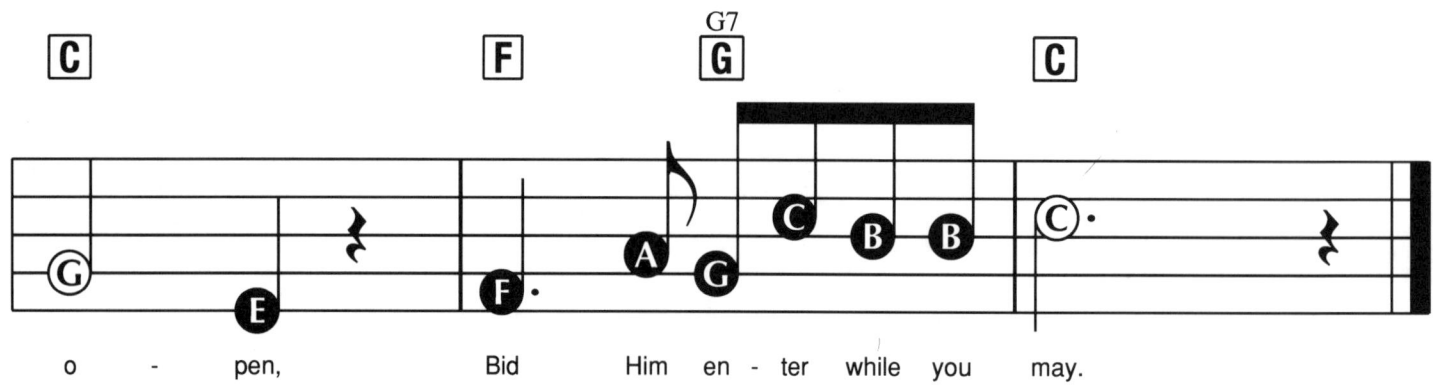

Praise God, From Whom All Blessings Flow

Praise To God, Immortal Praise

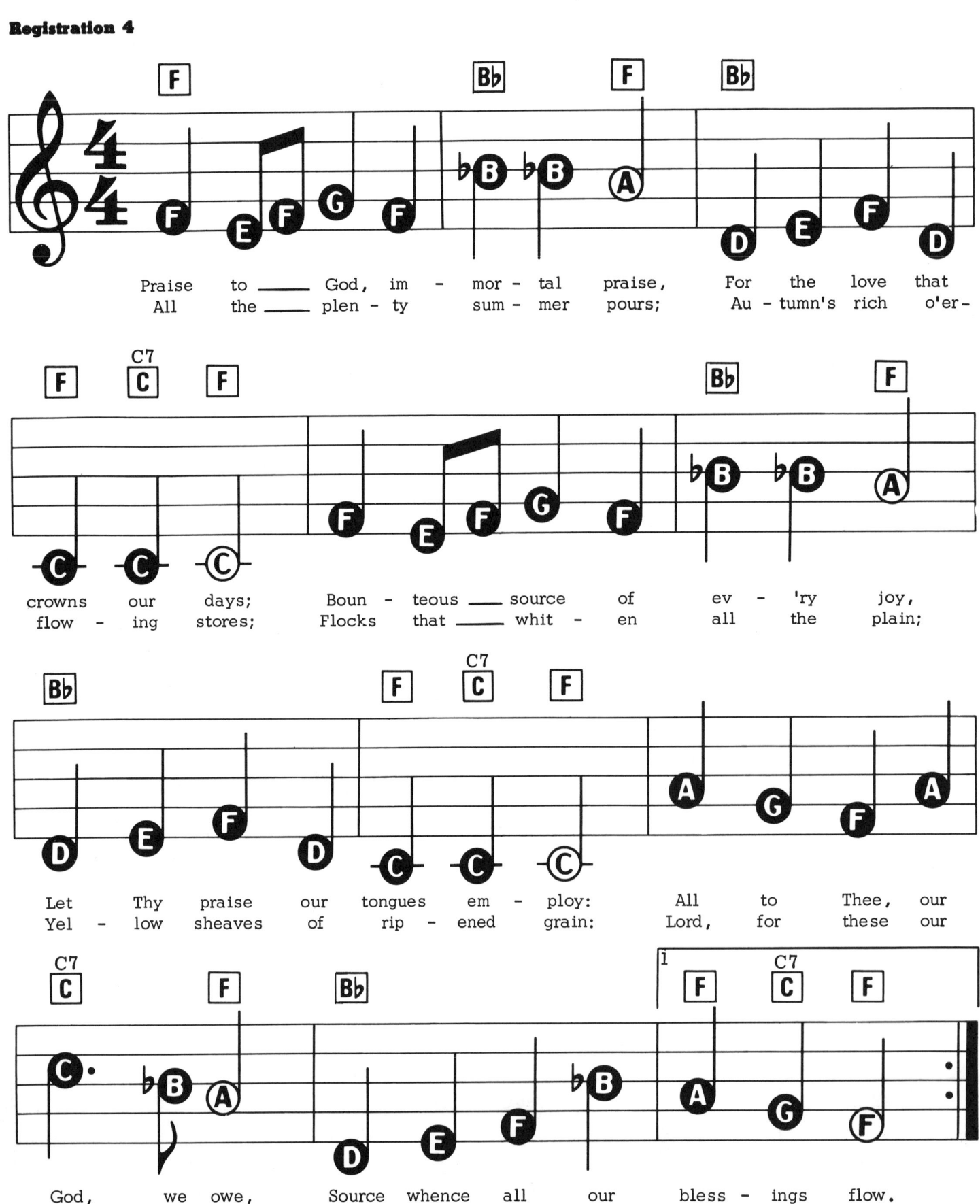

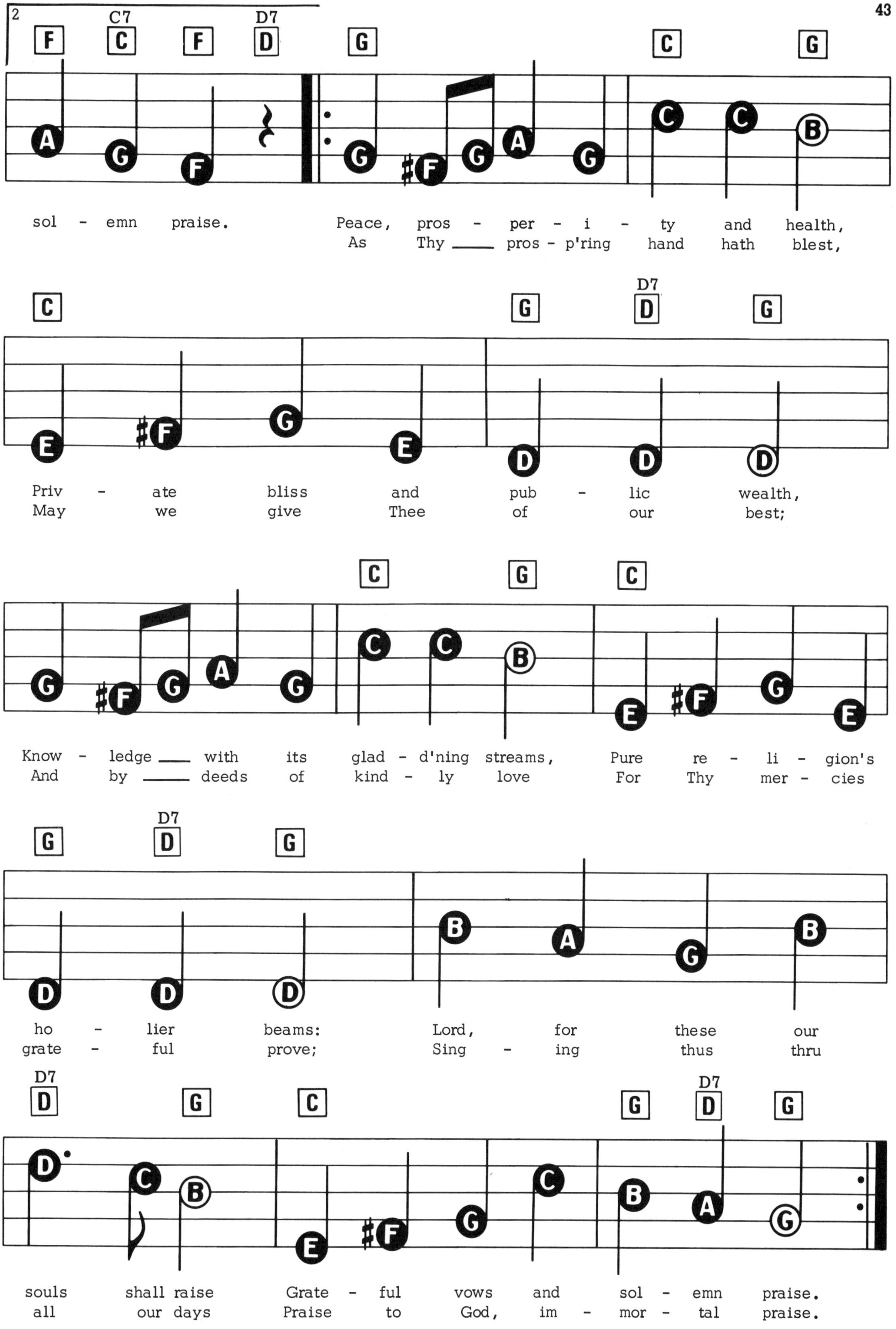

Rise Up, Oh Men Of God

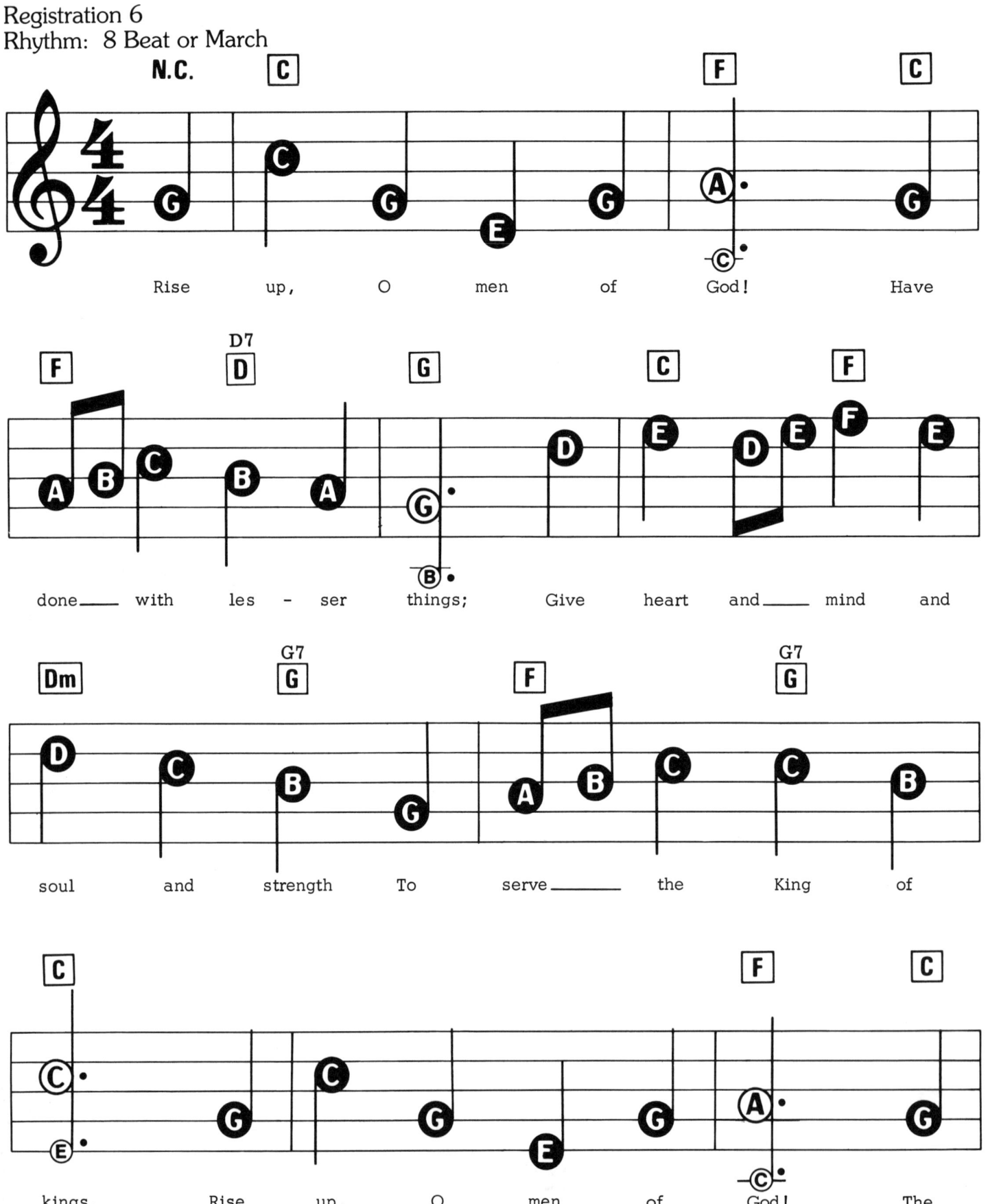

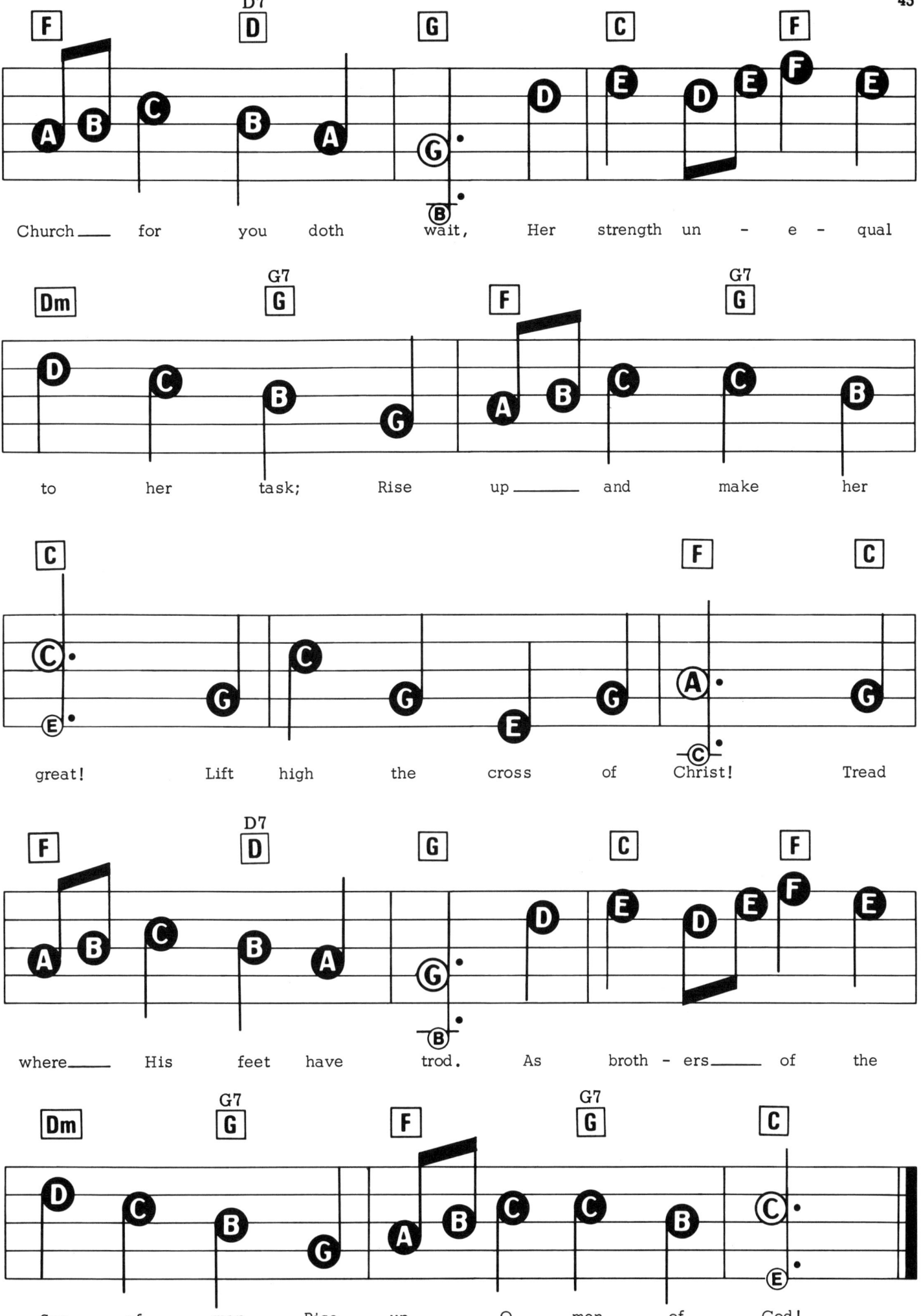

Rock Of Ages

Registration 6

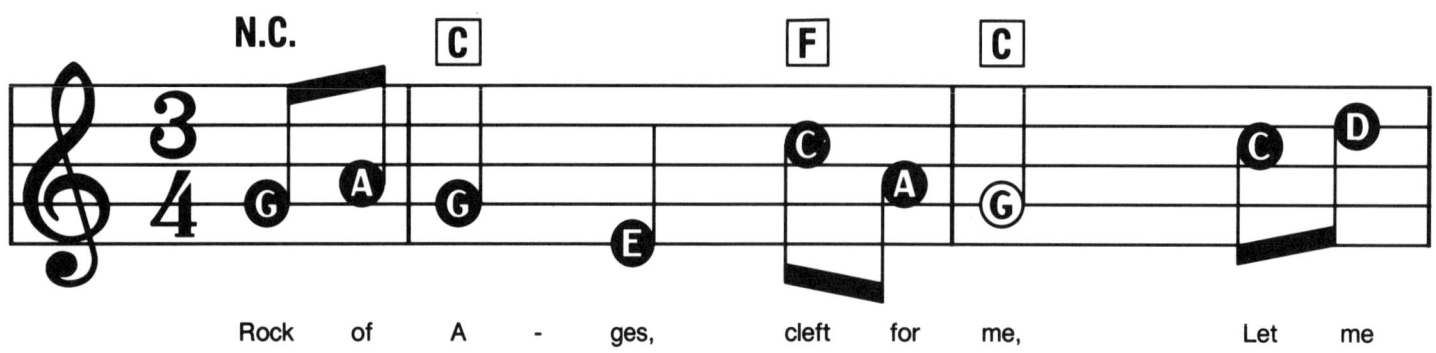
Rock of A - ges, cleft for me, Let me

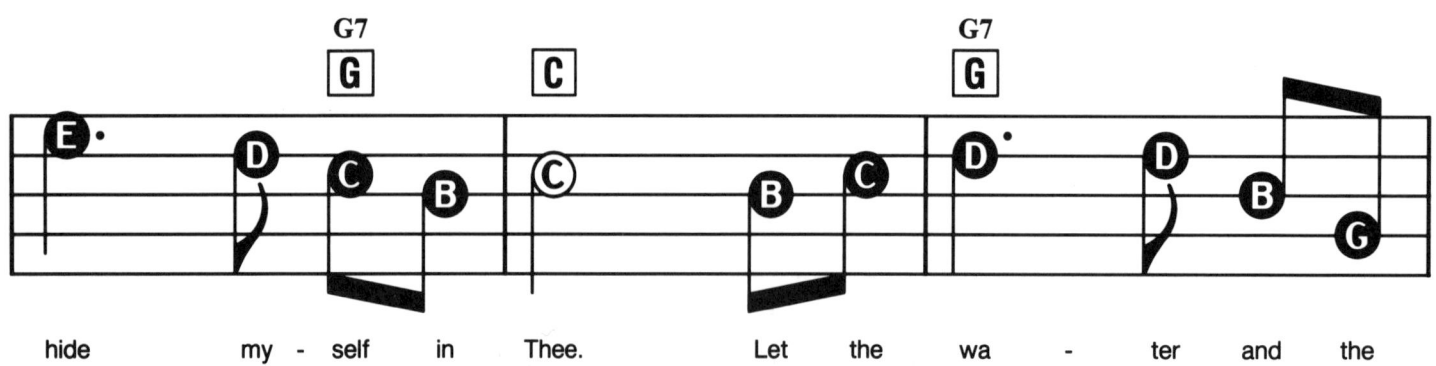
hide my - self in Thee. Let the wa - ter and the

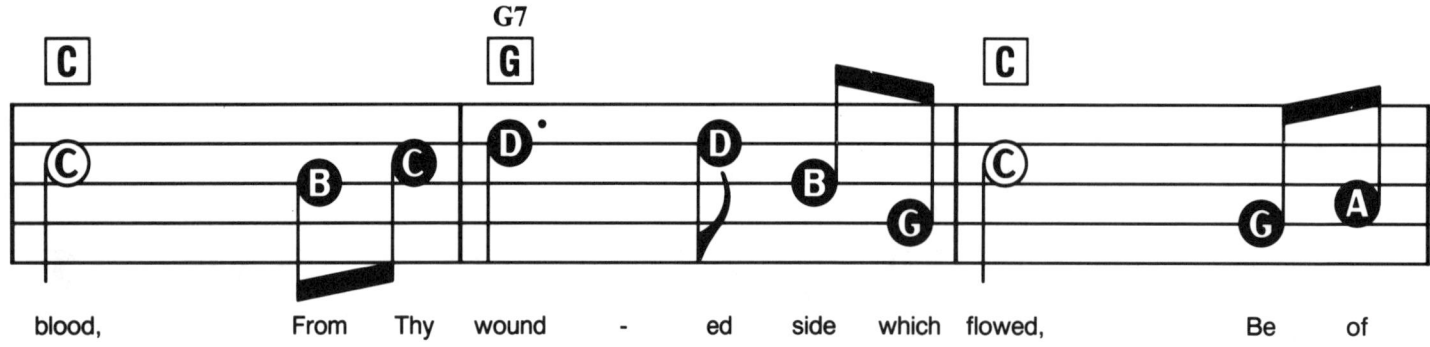
blood, From Thy wound - ed side which flowed, Be of

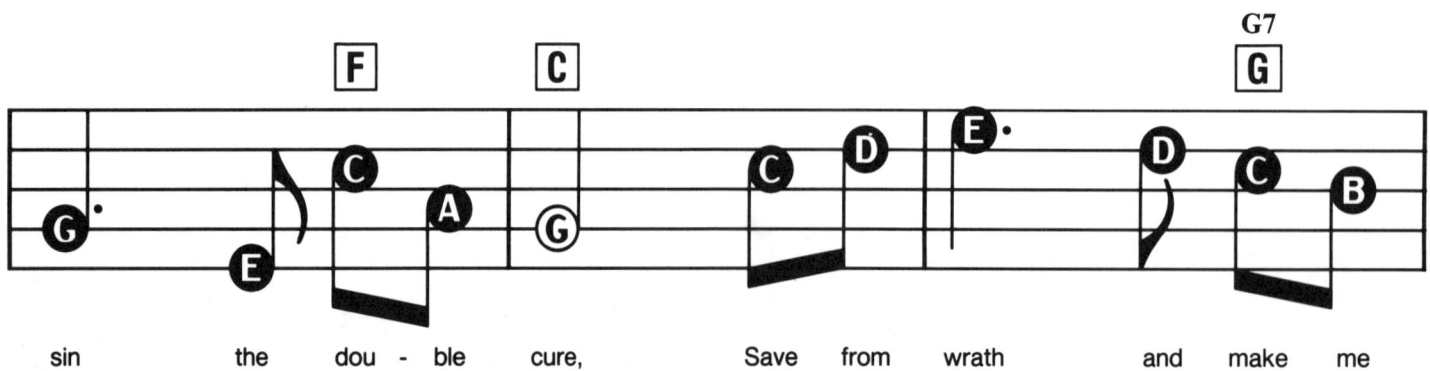
sin the dou - ble cure, Save from wrath and make me

Send The Light

Registration 3
Rhythm: 6/8 March

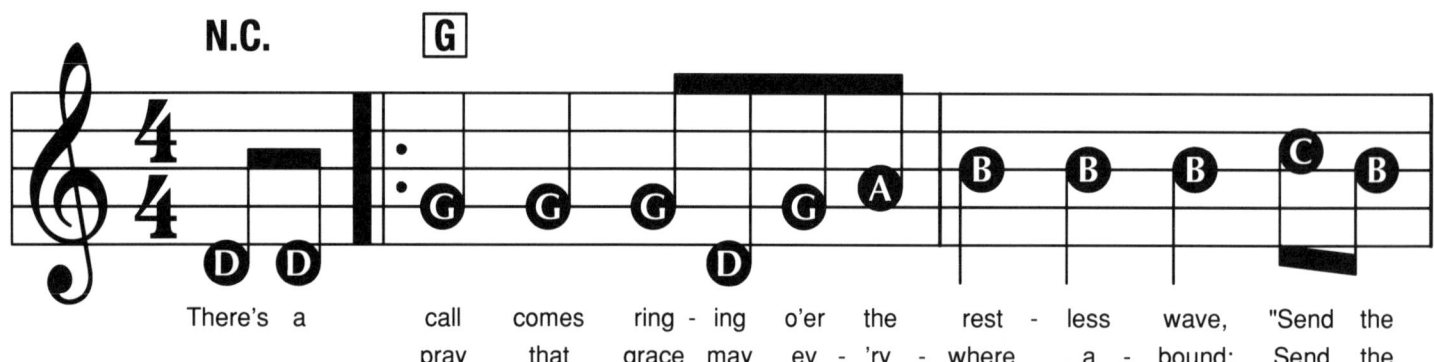

There's a call comes ring - ing o'er the rest - less wave, "Send the
pray that grace may ev - 'ry - where a - bound; Send the

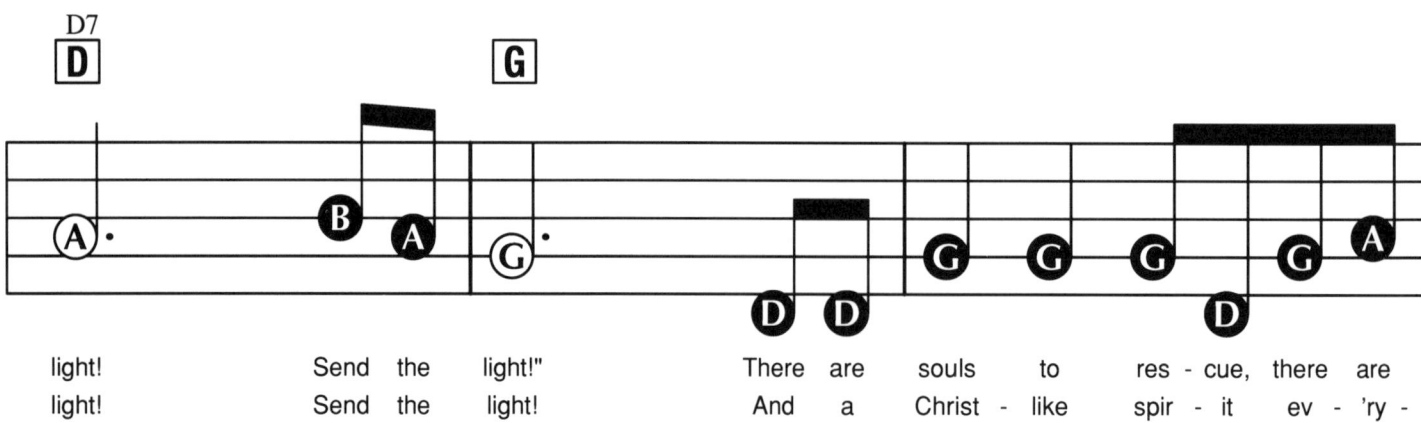

light! Send the light!" There are souls to res - cue, there are
light! Send the light! And a Christ - like spir - it ev - 'ry -

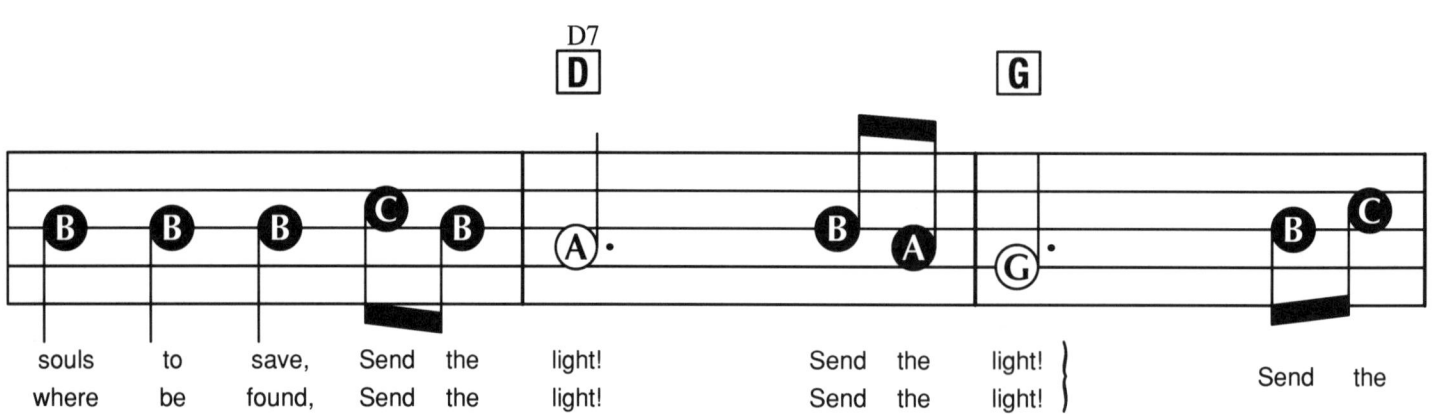

souls to save, Send the light! Send the light! Send the
where be found, Send the light! Send the light!

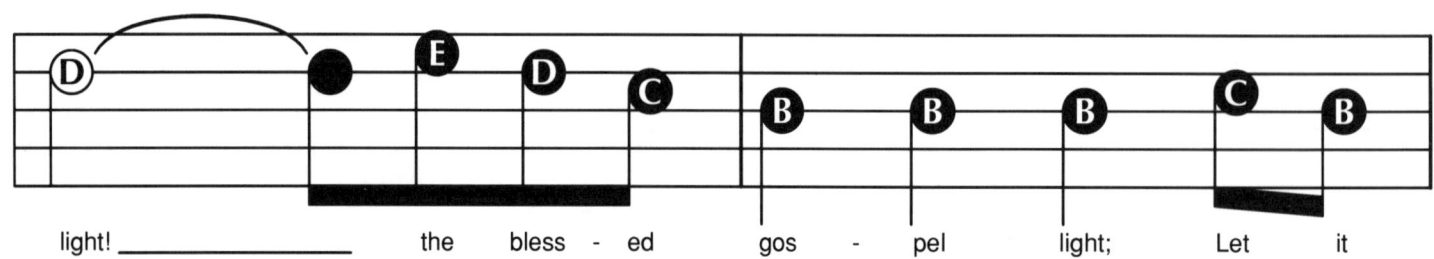

light! _____ the bless - ed gos - pel light; Let it

Copyright © 1991 by HAL LEONARD PUBLISHING CORPORATION
International Copyright Secured   All Rights Reserved

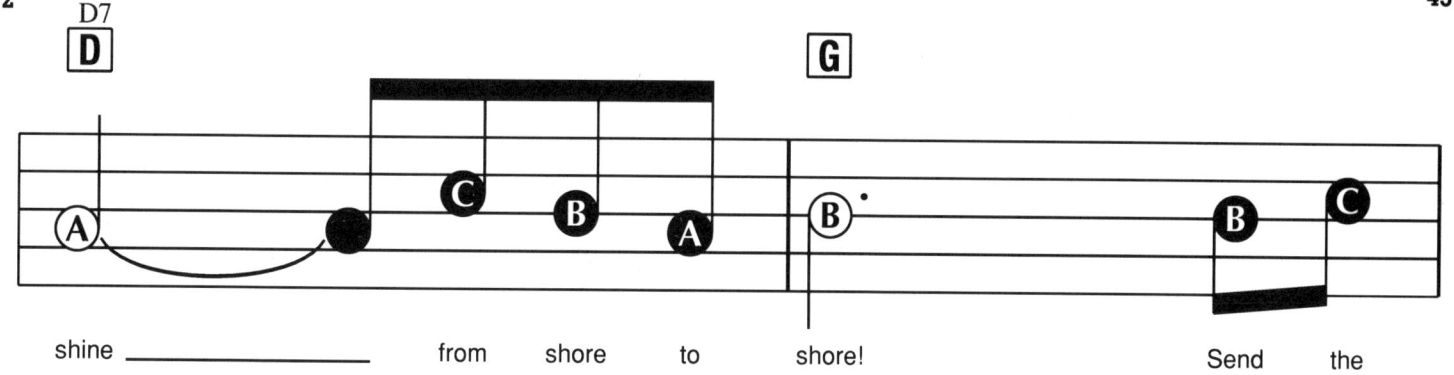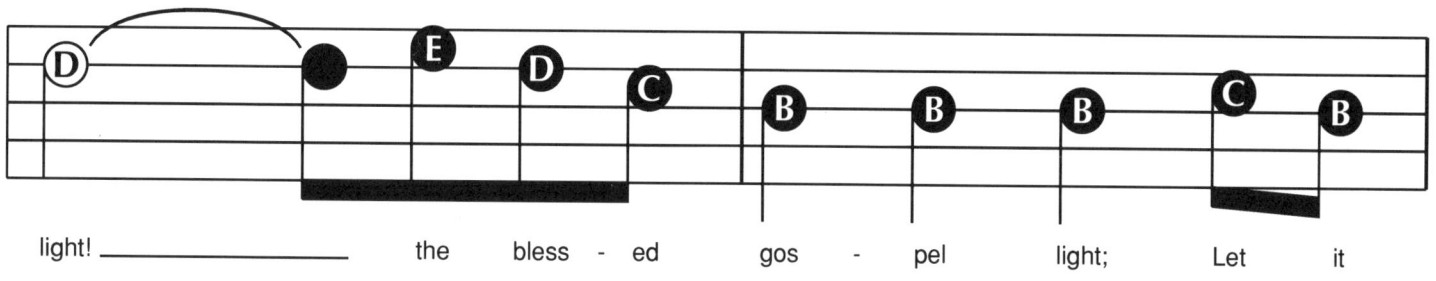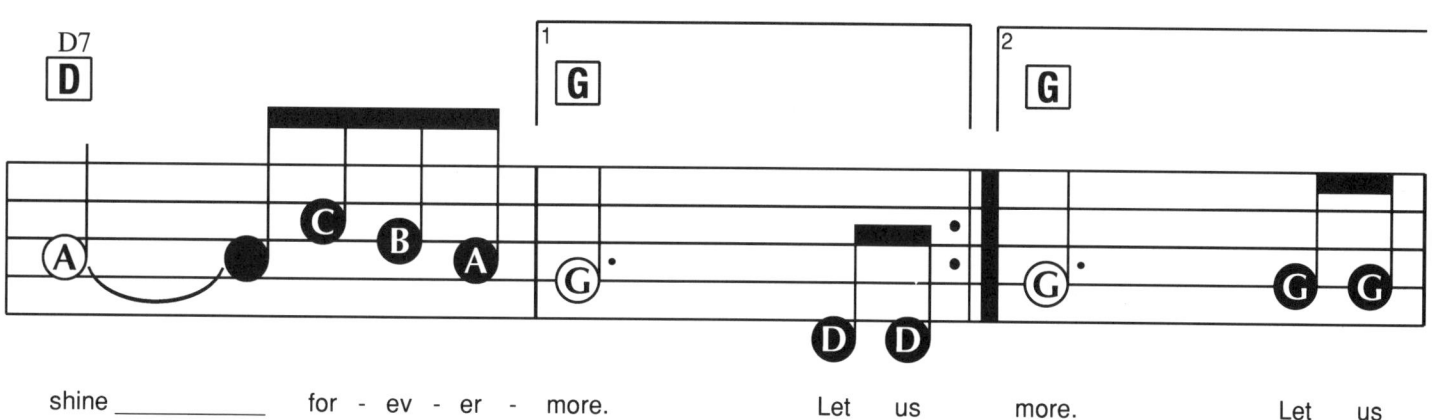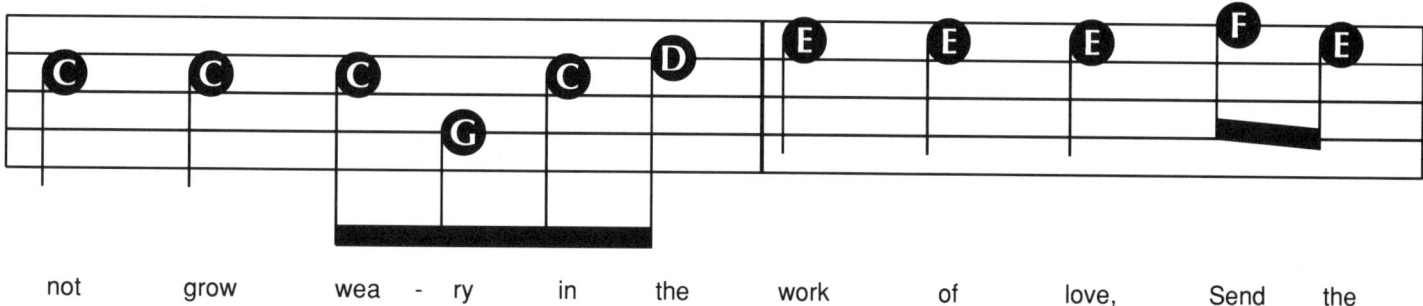

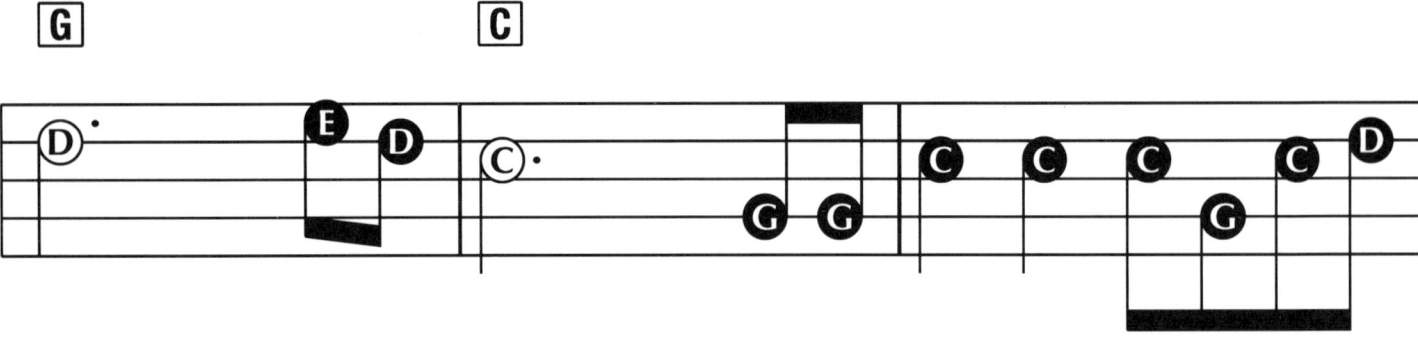
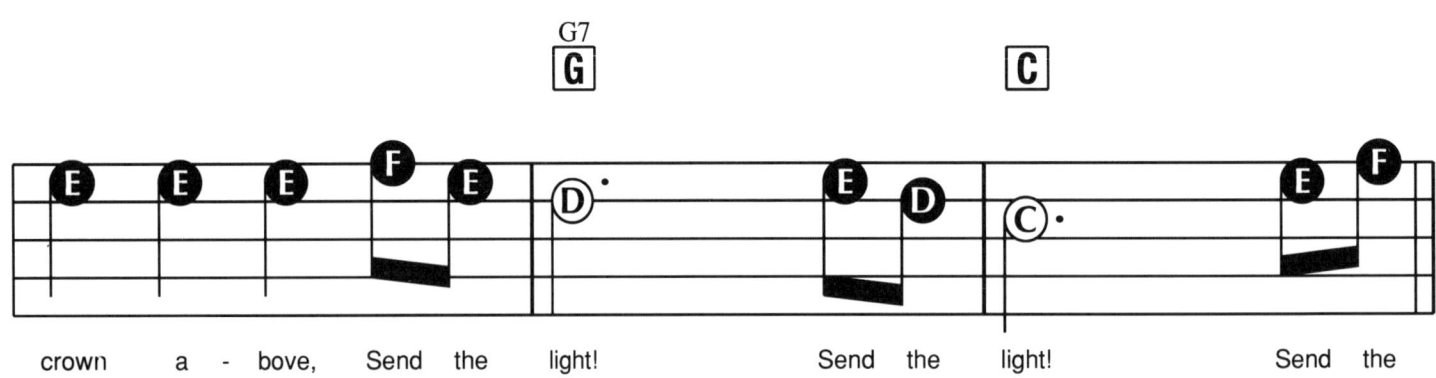
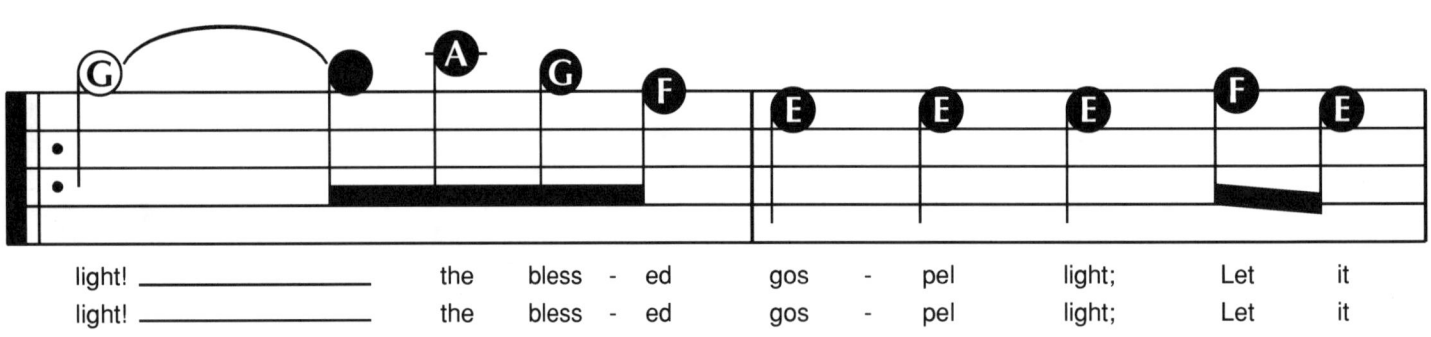
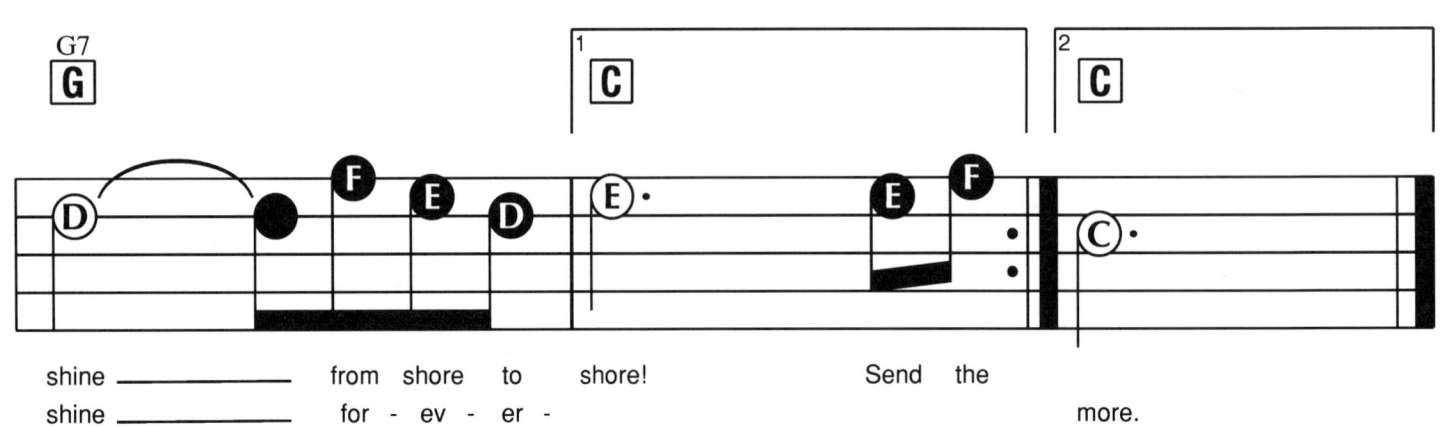

There Is Power In The Blood

Registration 2
Rhythm: March

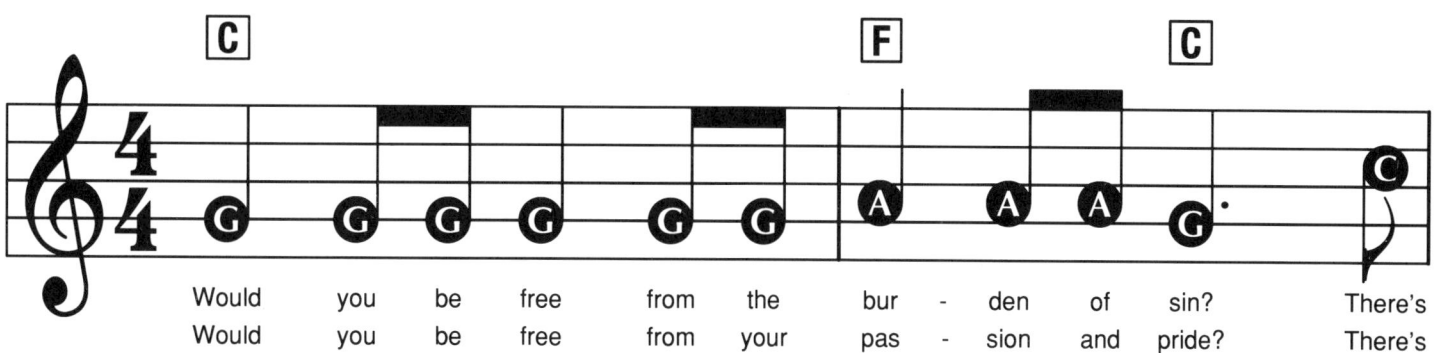

Would you be free from the bur - den of sin? There's
Would you be free from your pas - sion and pride? There's

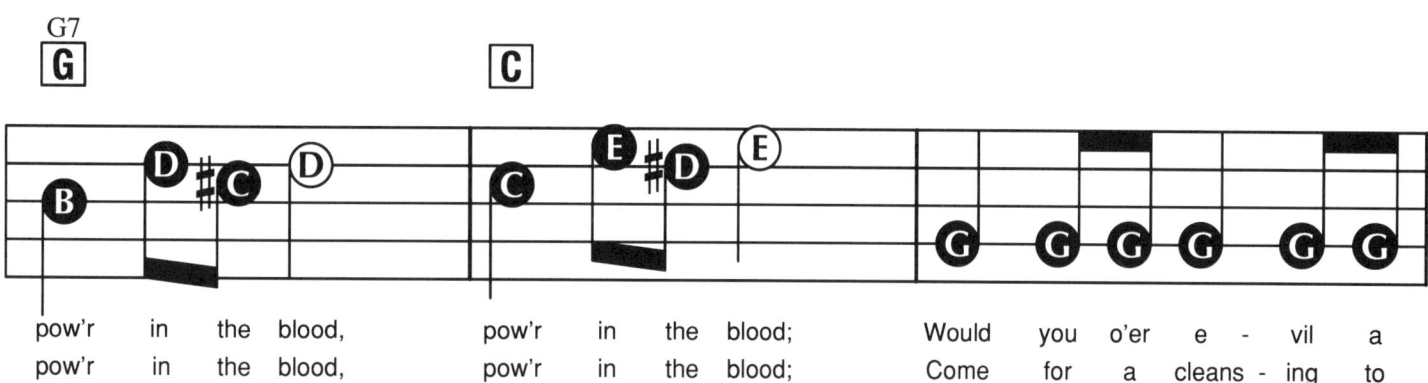

pow'r in the blood, pow'r in the blood; Would you o'er e - vil a
pow'r in the blood, pow'r in the blood; Come for a cleans - ing to

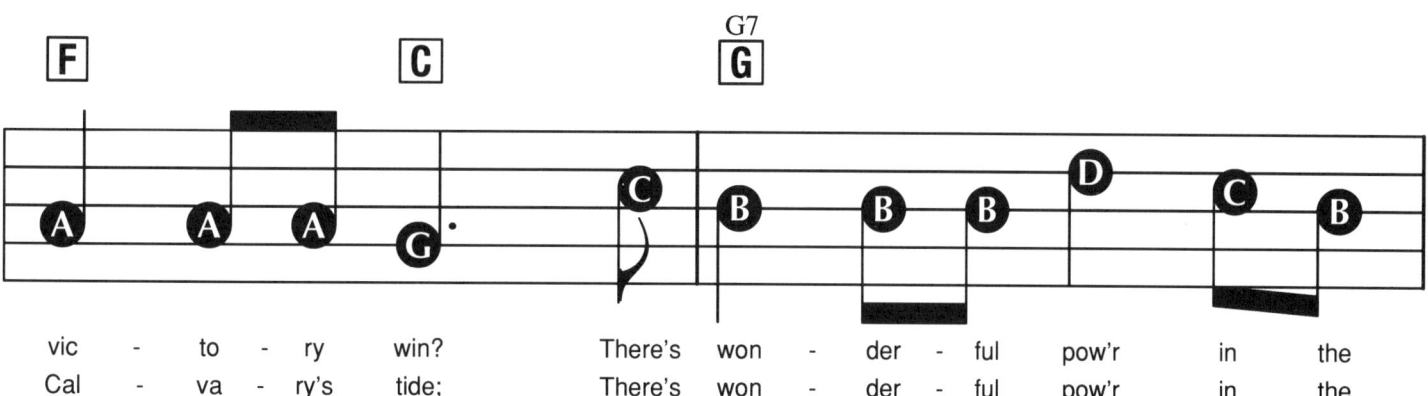

vic - to - ry win? There's won - der - ful pow'r in the
Cal - va - ry's tide; There's won - der - ful pow'r in the

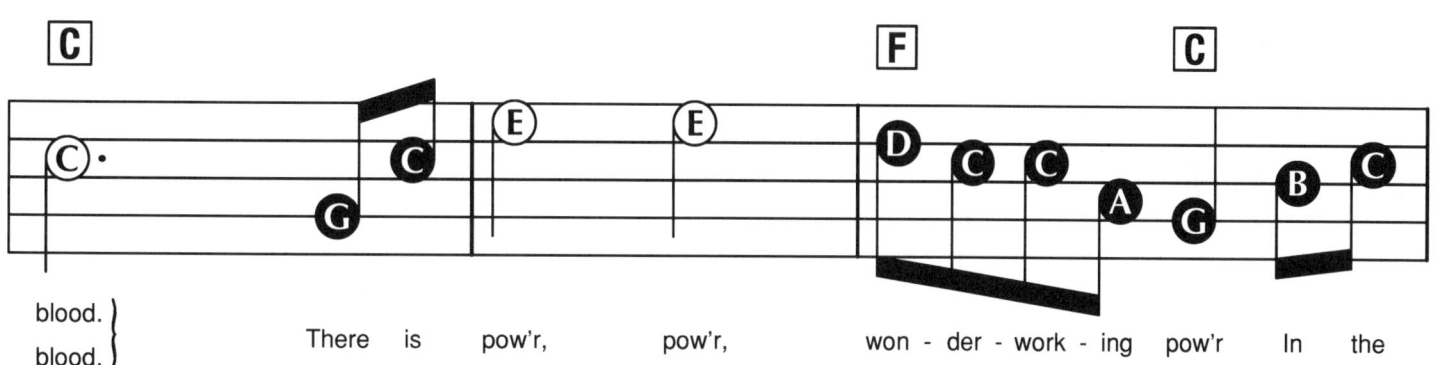

blood. }
blood. } There is pow'r, pow'r, won - der - work - ing pow'r In the

Copyright © 1991 by HAL LEONARD PUBLISHING CORPORATION
International Copyright Secured All Rights Reserved

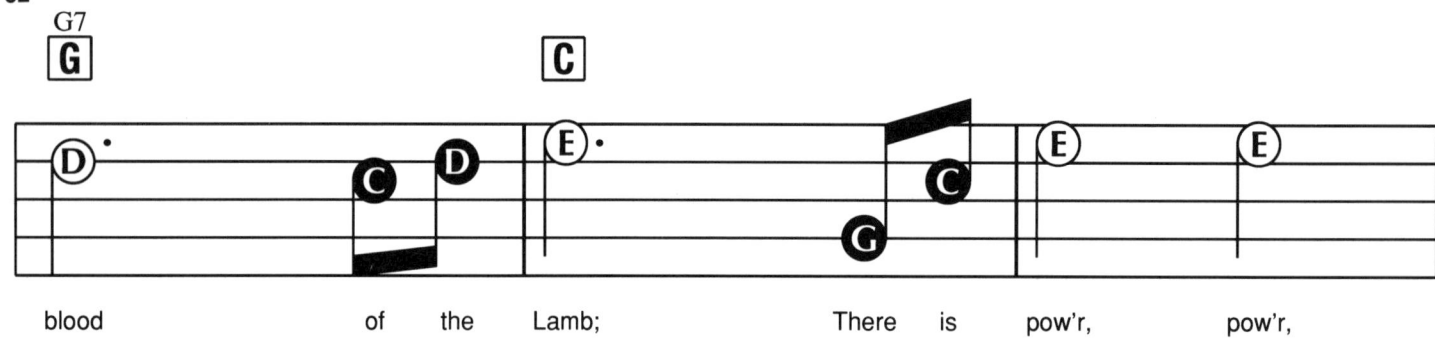
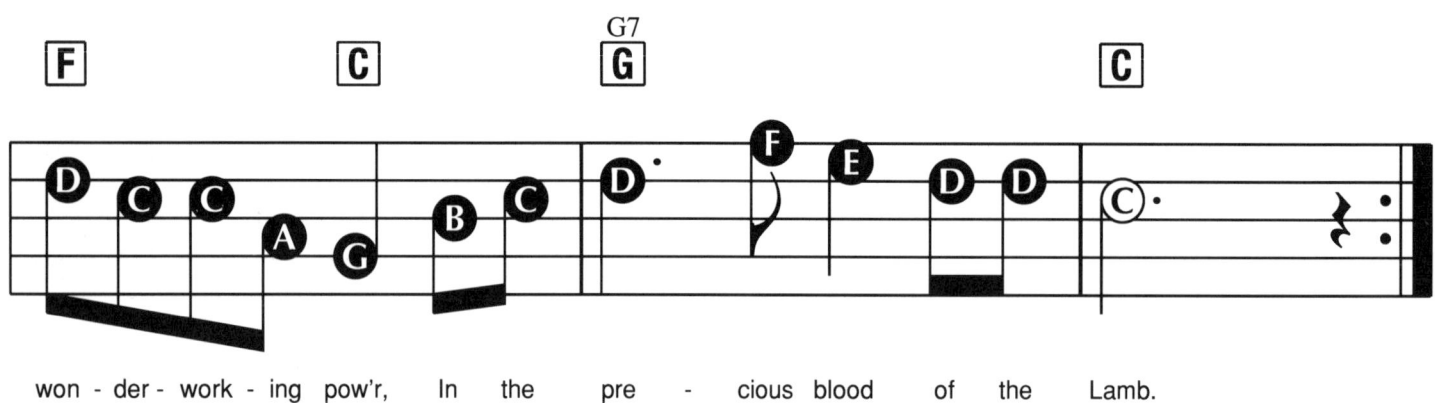
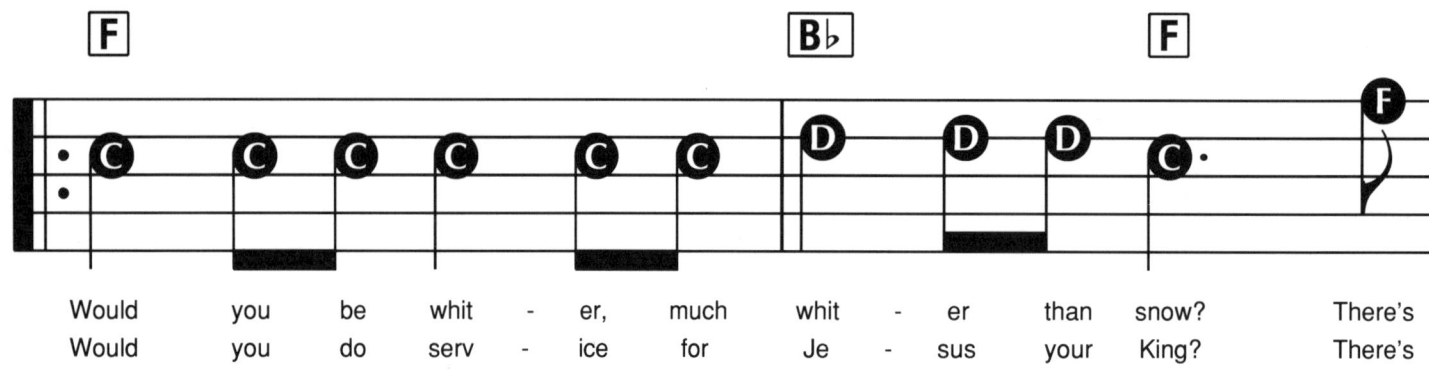
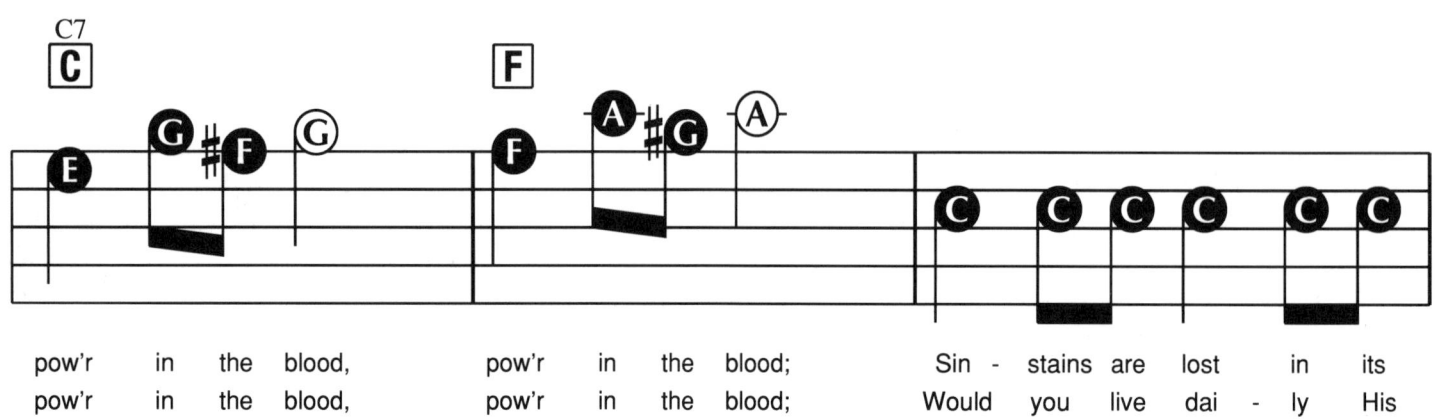

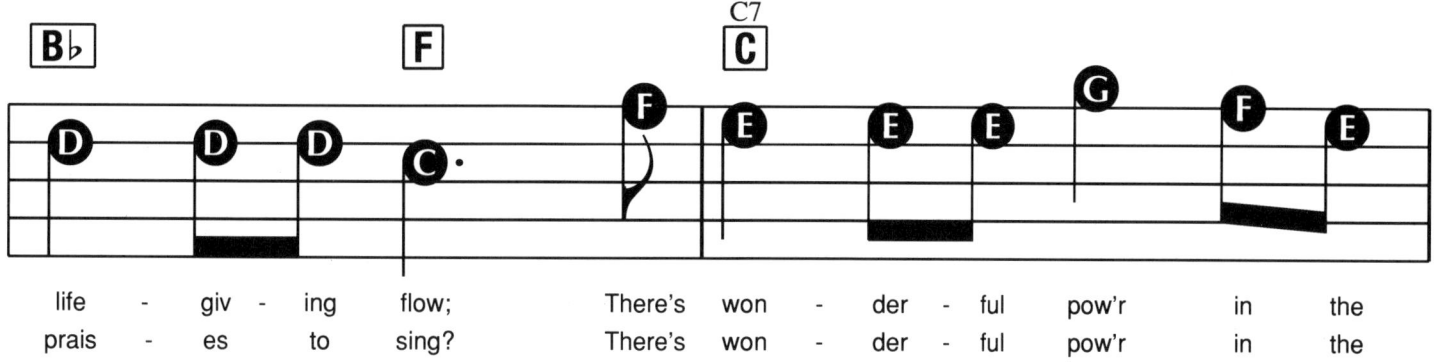
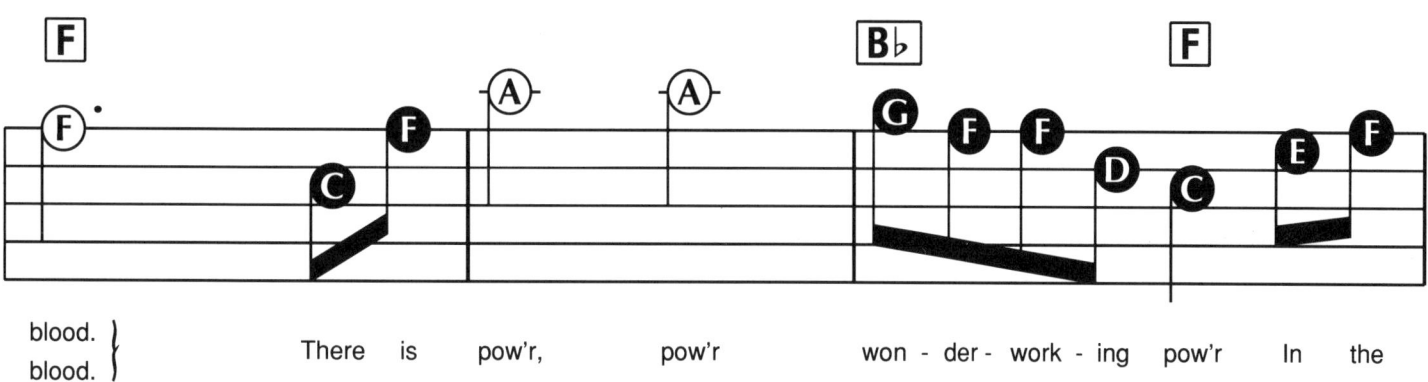
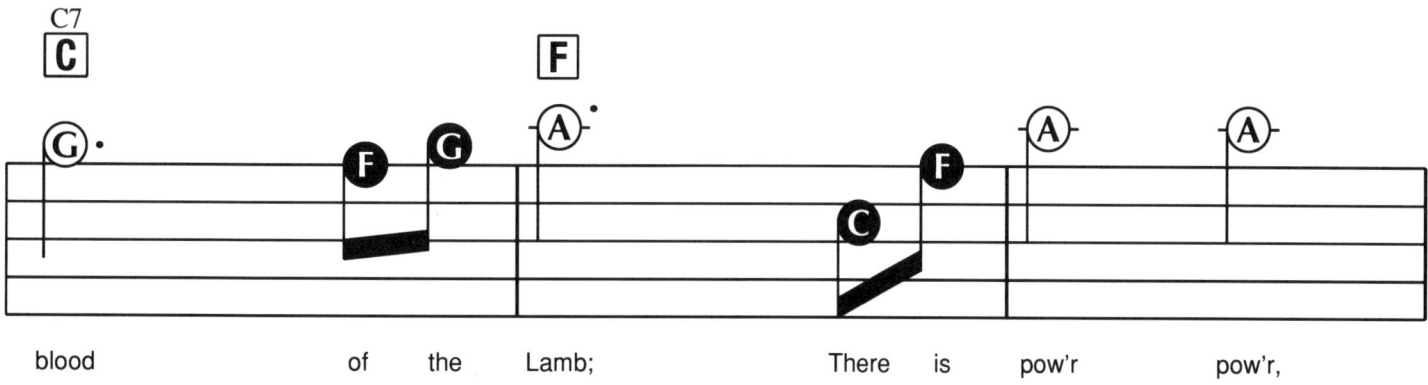
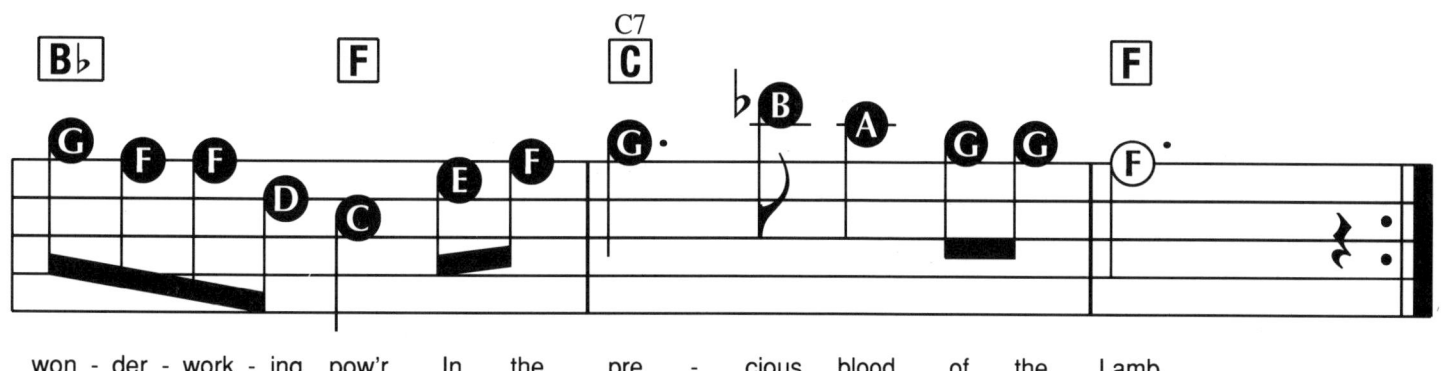

Tell Me The Old, Old Story

Registration 5
Rhythm: 8 Beat or March

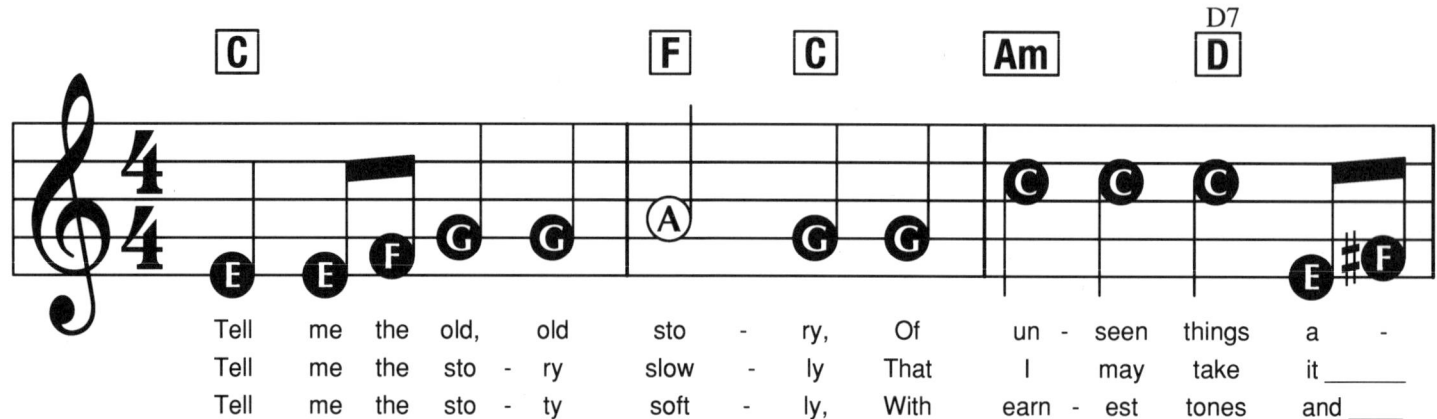

Tell me the old, old sto - ry, Of un - seen things a -
Tell me the sto - ry slow - ly That I may take it
Tell me the sto - ry soft - ly, With earn - est tones and

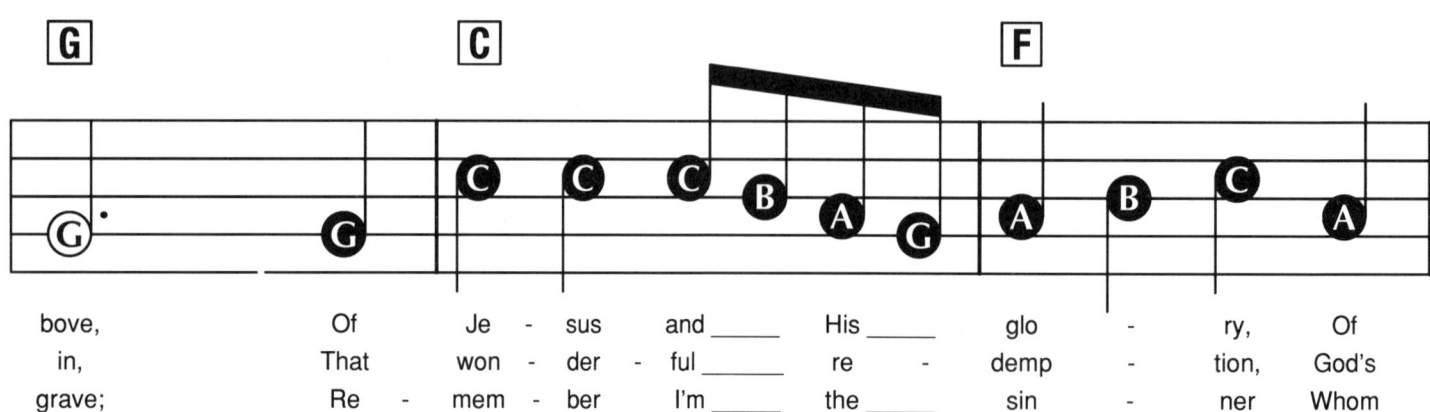

bove, Of Je - sus and His glo - ry, Of
in, That won - der - ful re - demp - tion, God's
grave; Re - mem - ber I'm the sin - ner Whom

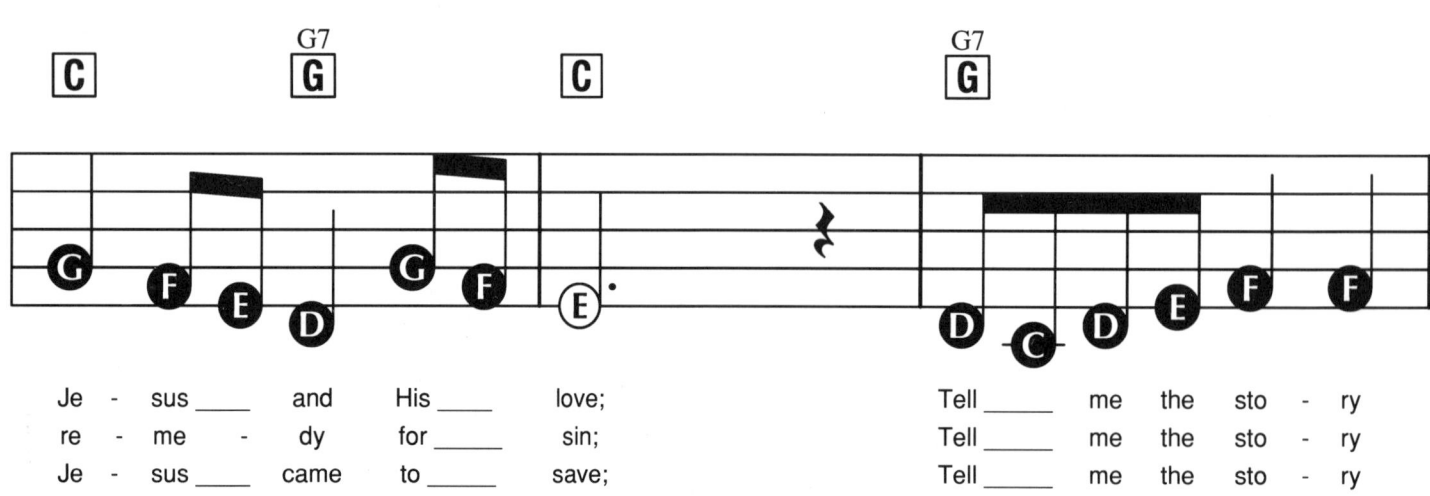

Je - sus and His love; Tell me the sto - ry
re - me - dy for sin; Tell me the sto - ry
Je - sus came to save; Tell me the sto - ry

Copyright © 1991 by HAL LEONARD PUBLISHING CORPORATION
International Copyright Secured   All Rights Reserved

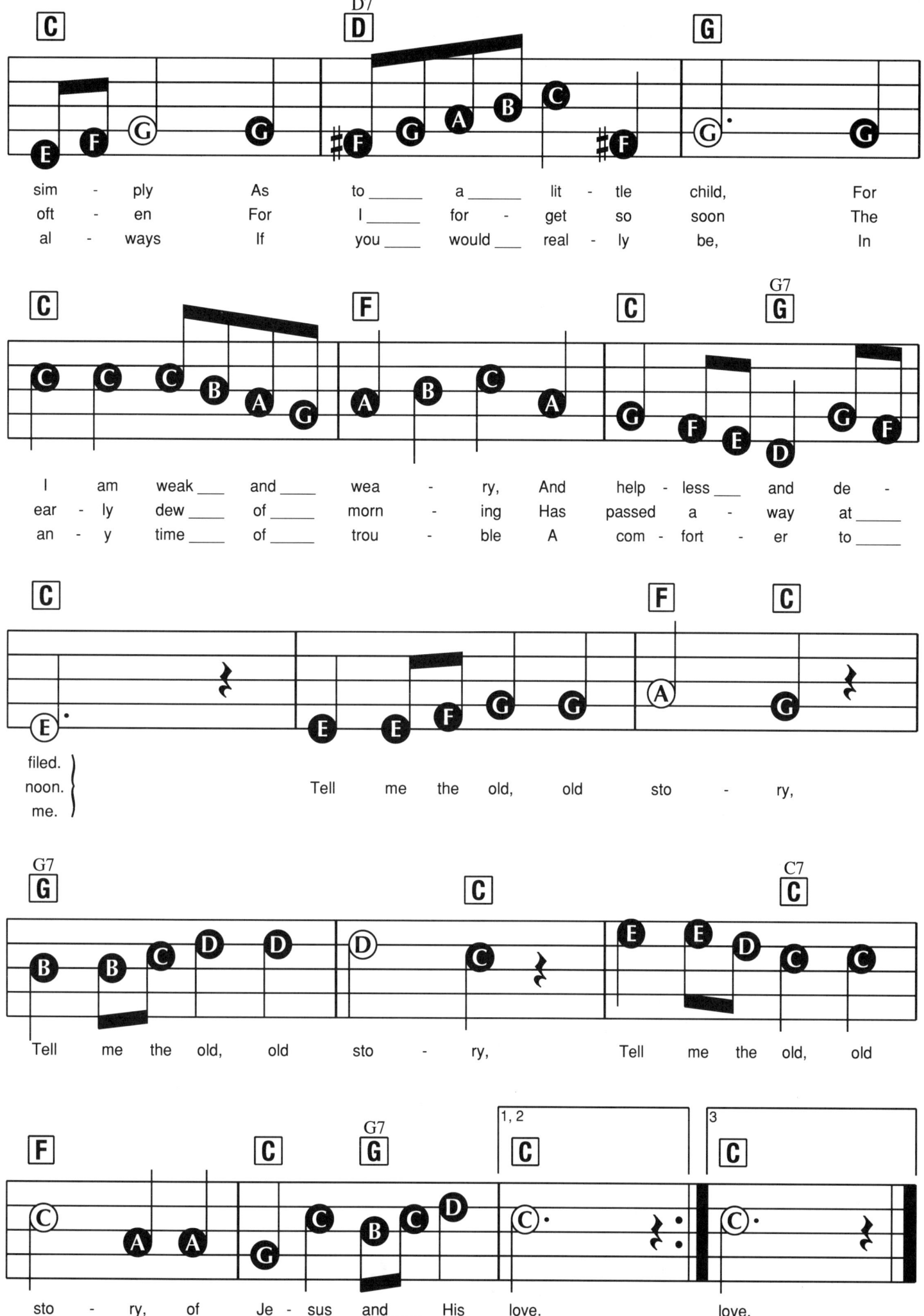

'Tis So Sweet To Trust In Jesus

Registration 4
Rhythm: 8 Beat

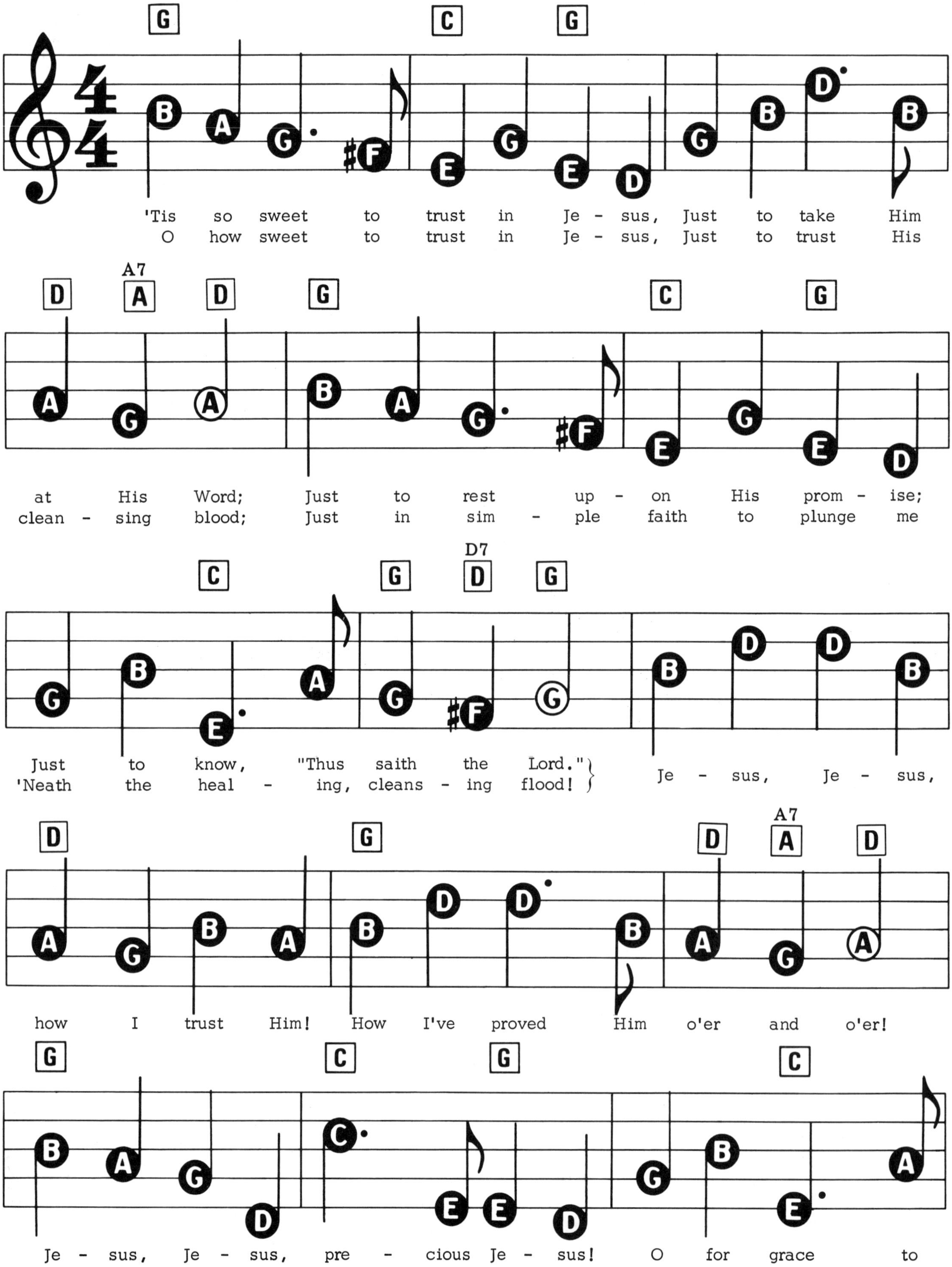

'Tis so sweet to trust in Je-sus, Just to take Him
O how sweet to trust in Je-sus, Just to trust His

at His Word; Just to rest up-on His prom-ise;
clean-sing blood; Just in sim-ple faith to plunge me

Just to know, "Thus saith the Lord." } Je-sus, Je-sus,
'Neath the heal-ing, cleans-ing flood!

how I trust Him! How I've proved Him o'er and o'er!

Je-sus, Je-sus, pre-cious Je-sus! O for grace to

Copyright © 1991 by HAL LEONARD PUBLISHING CORPORATION
International Copyright Secured   All Rights Reserved

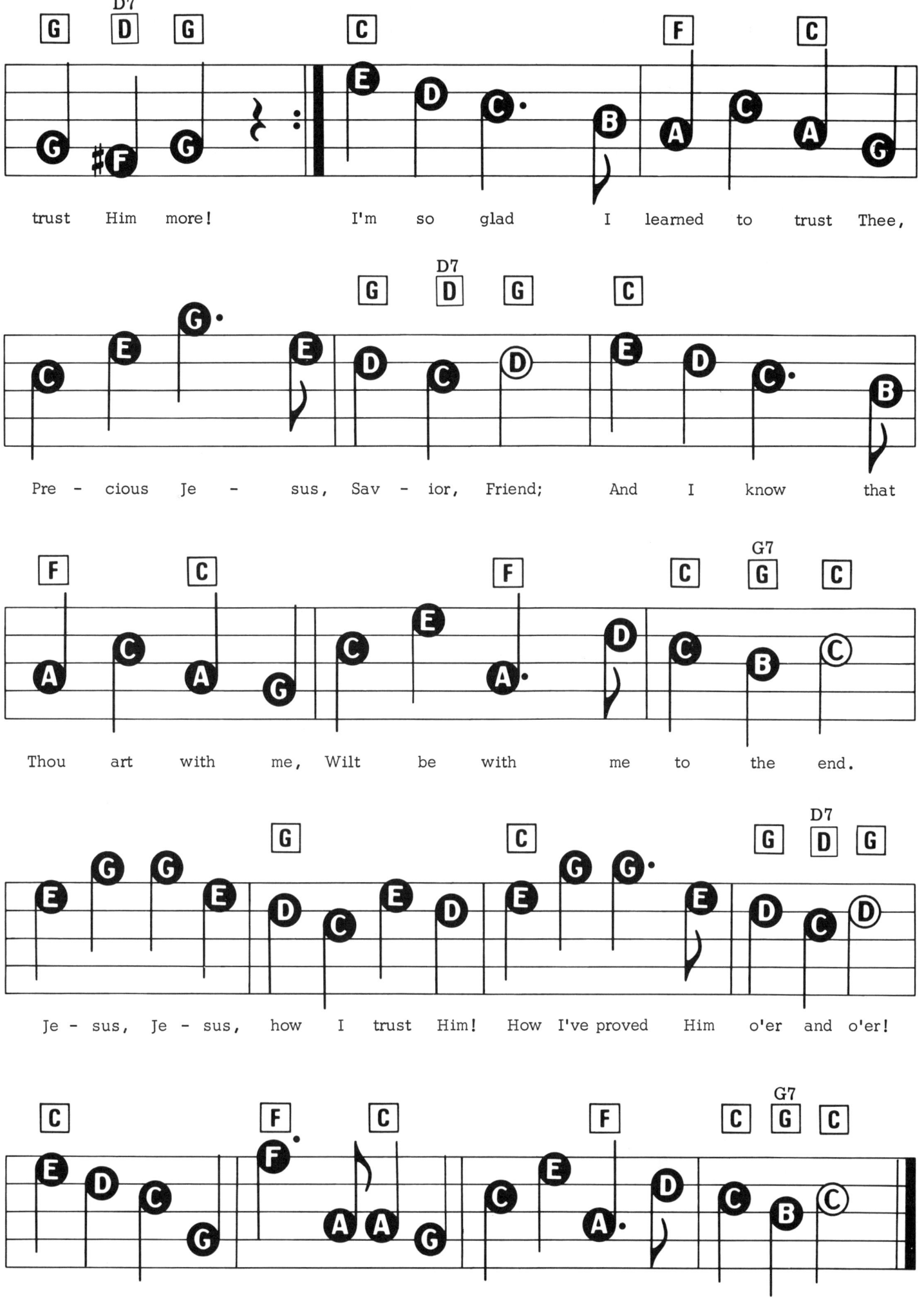

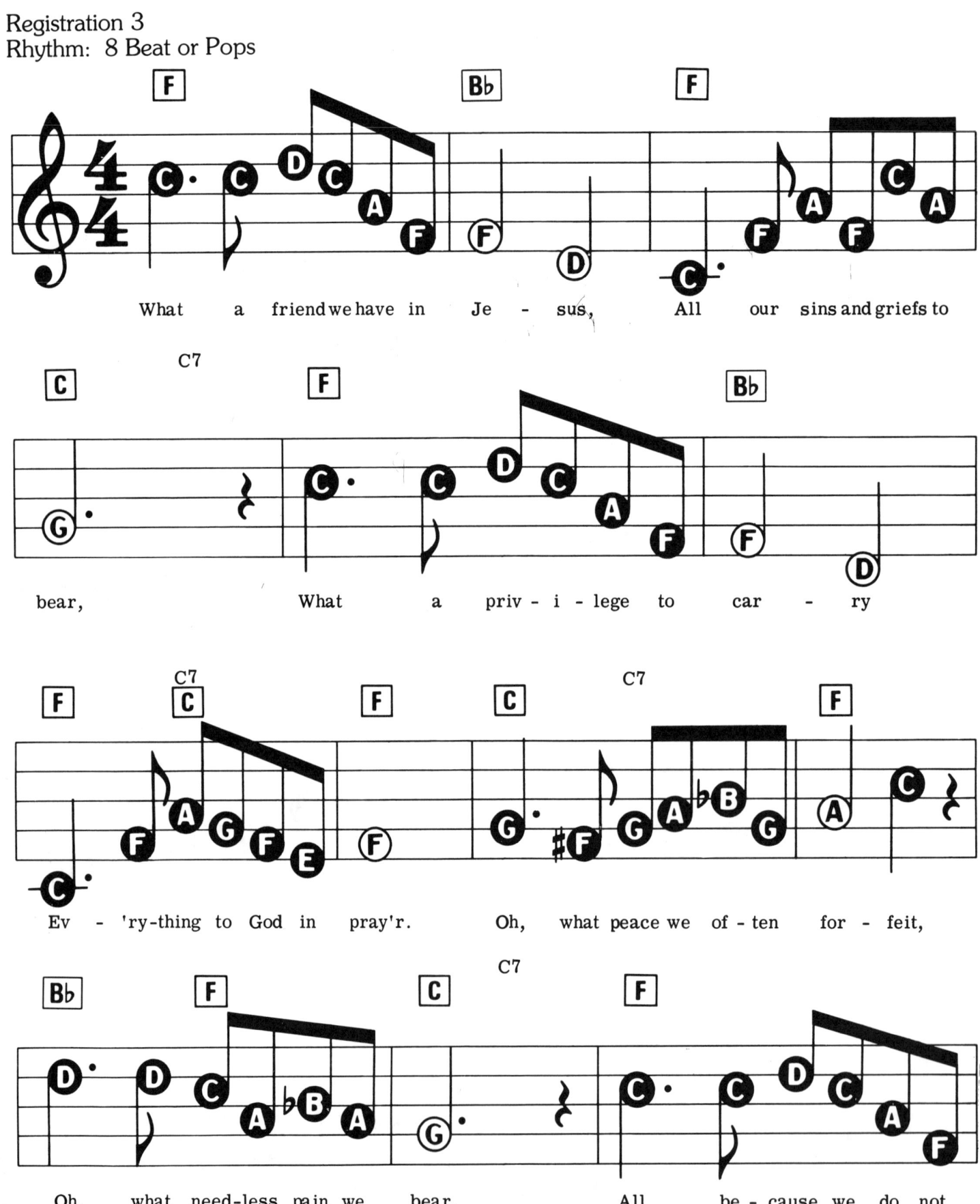

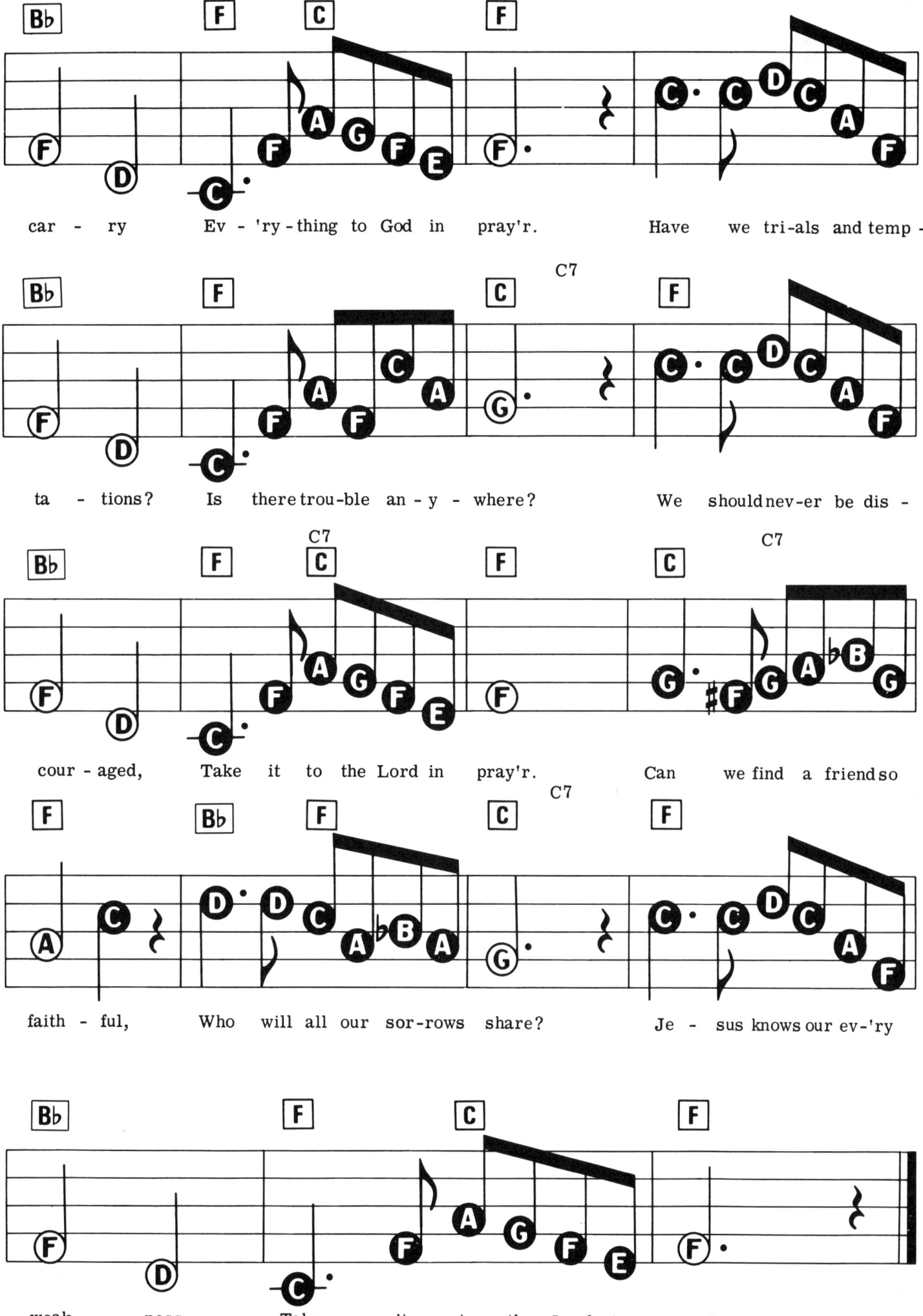

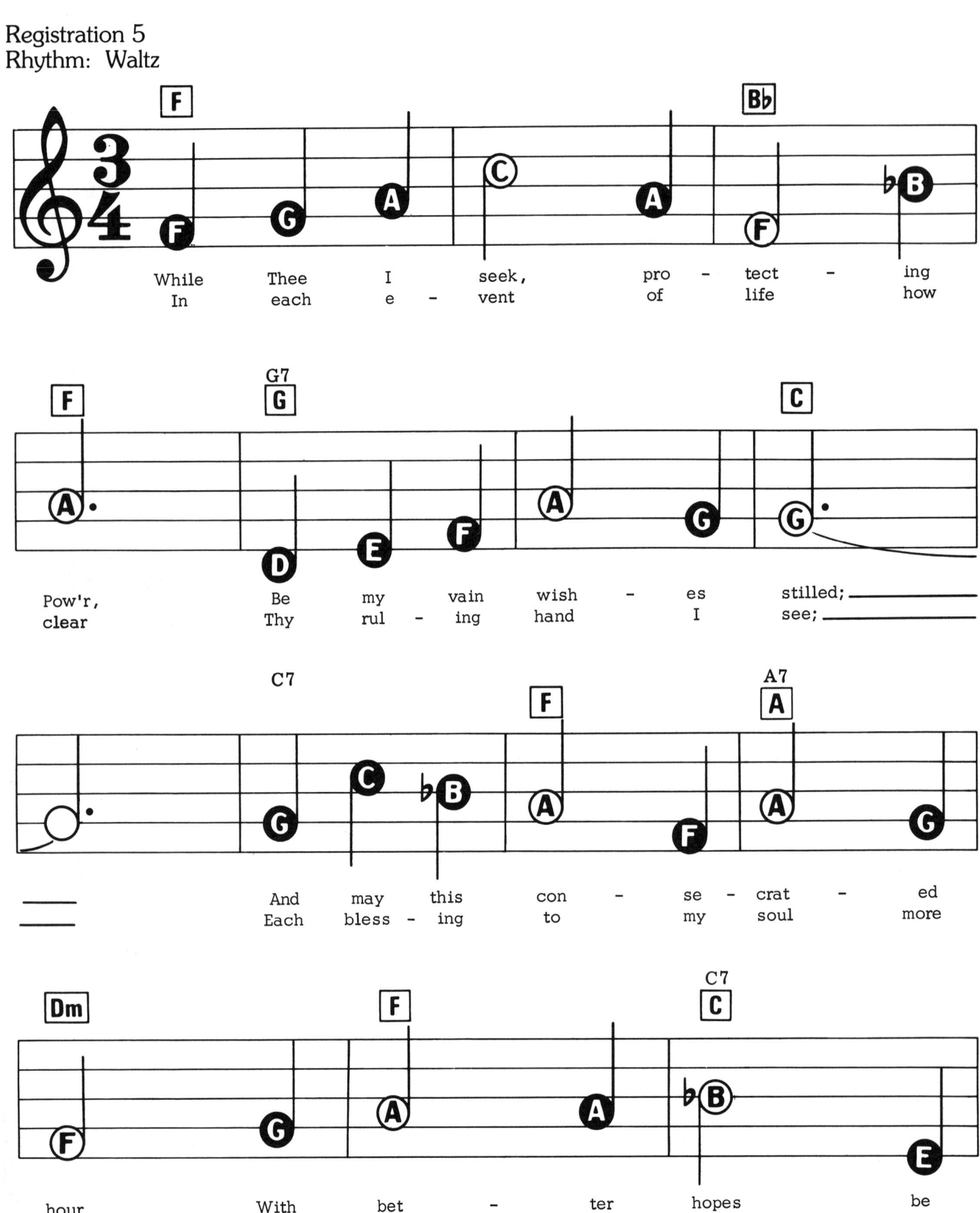

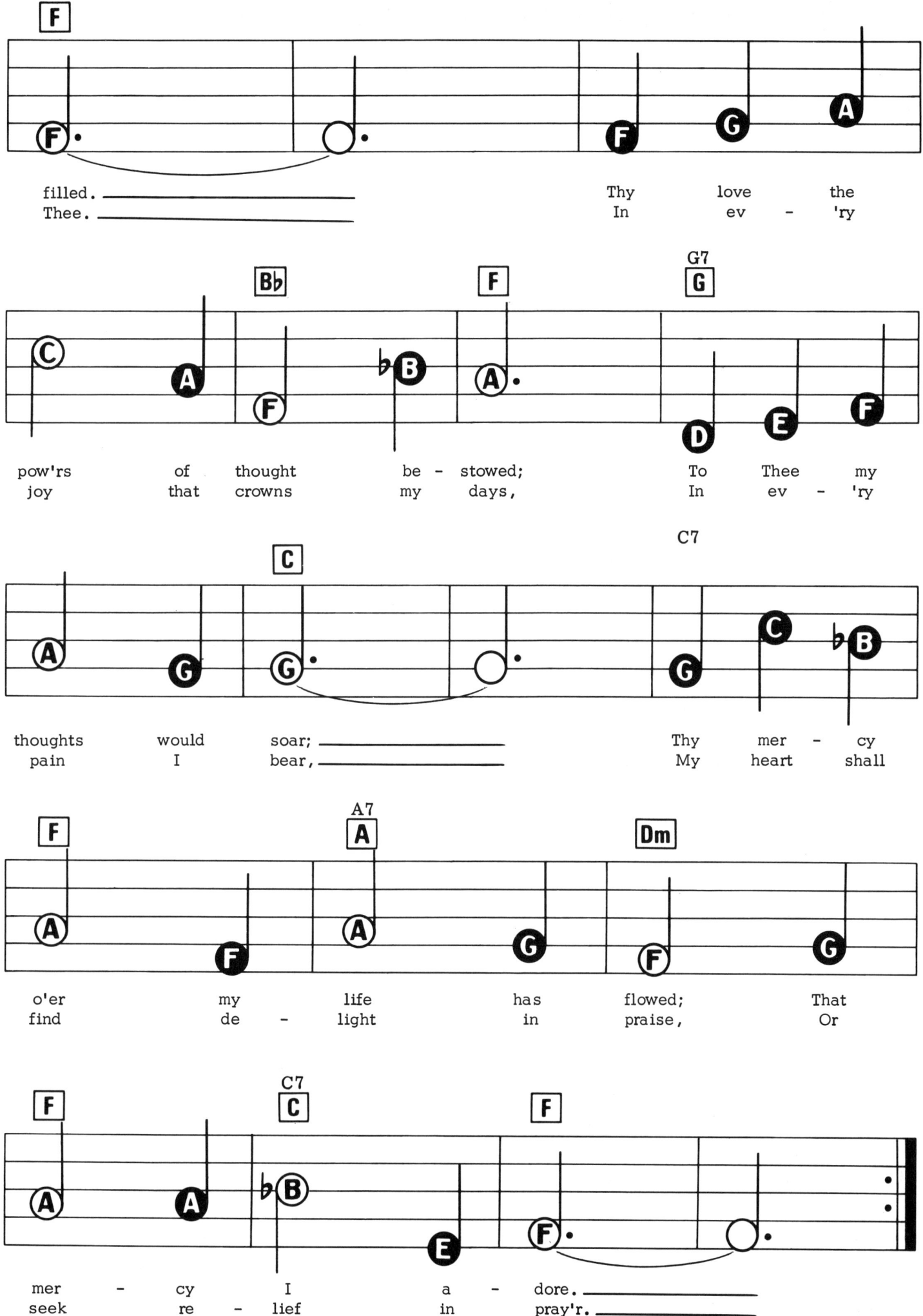

Wonderful Words Of Life

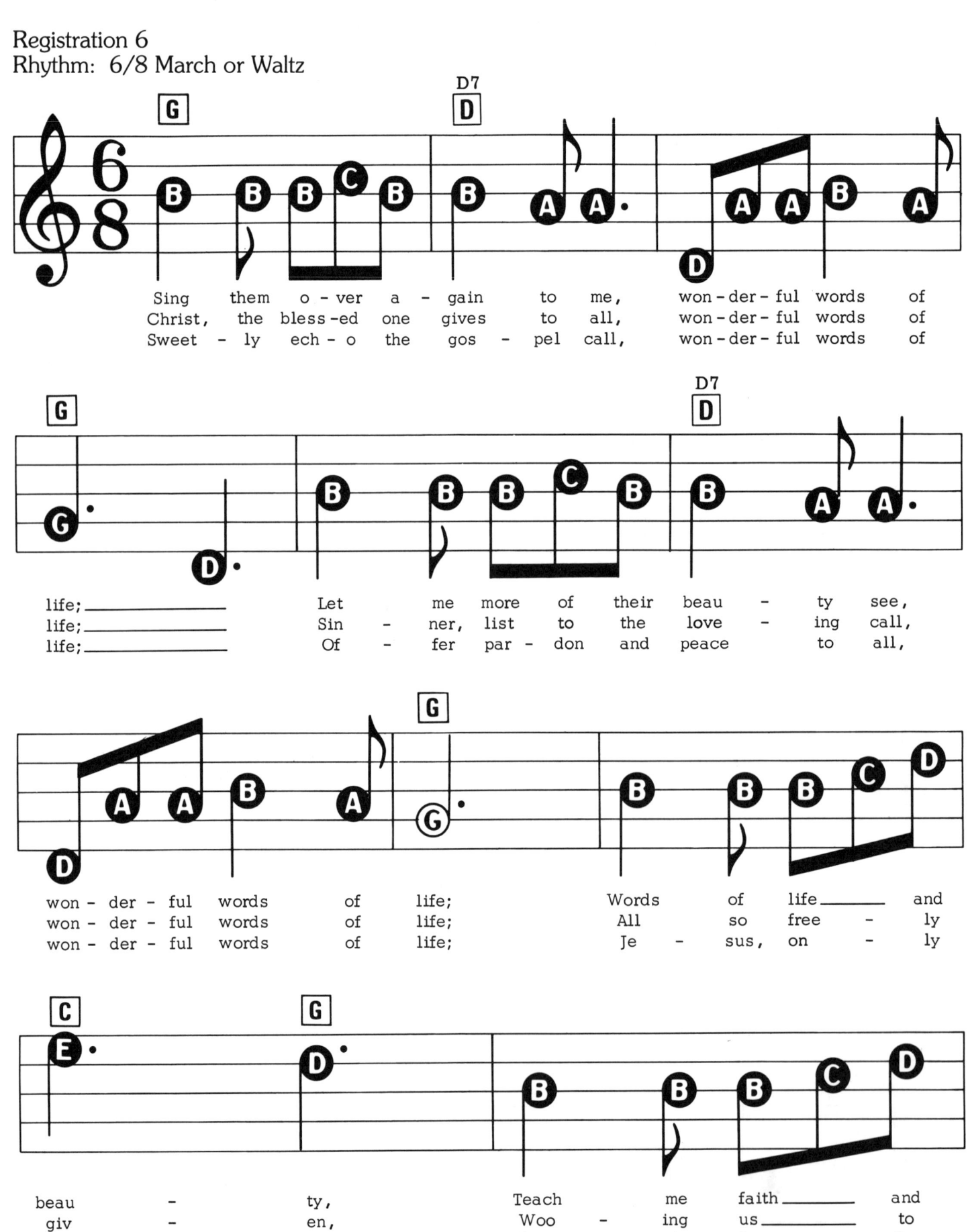

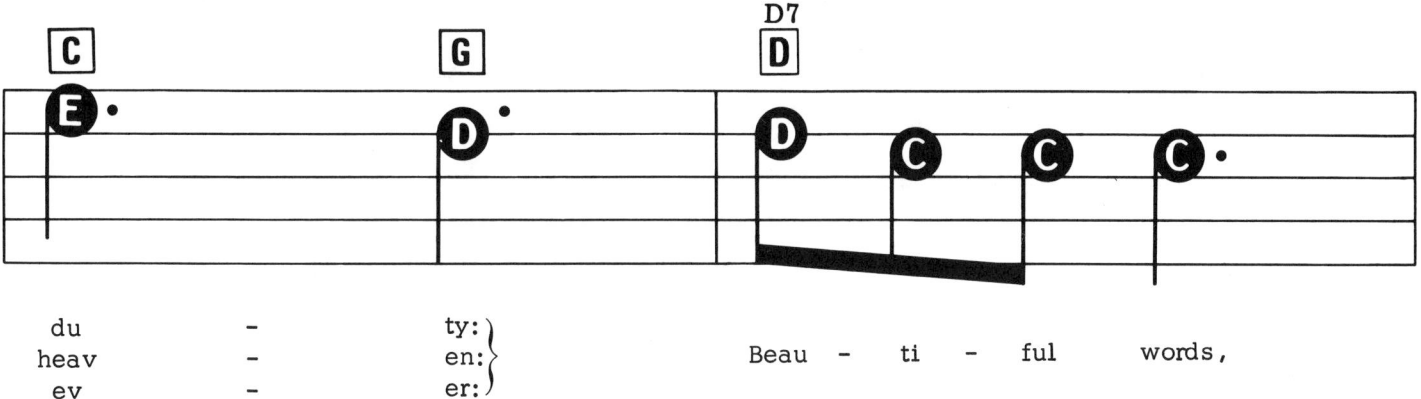
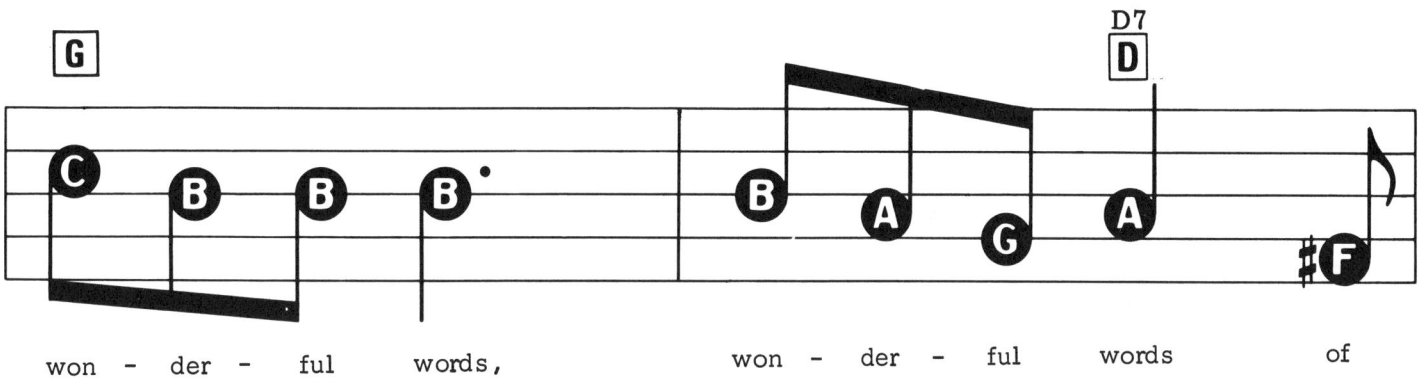
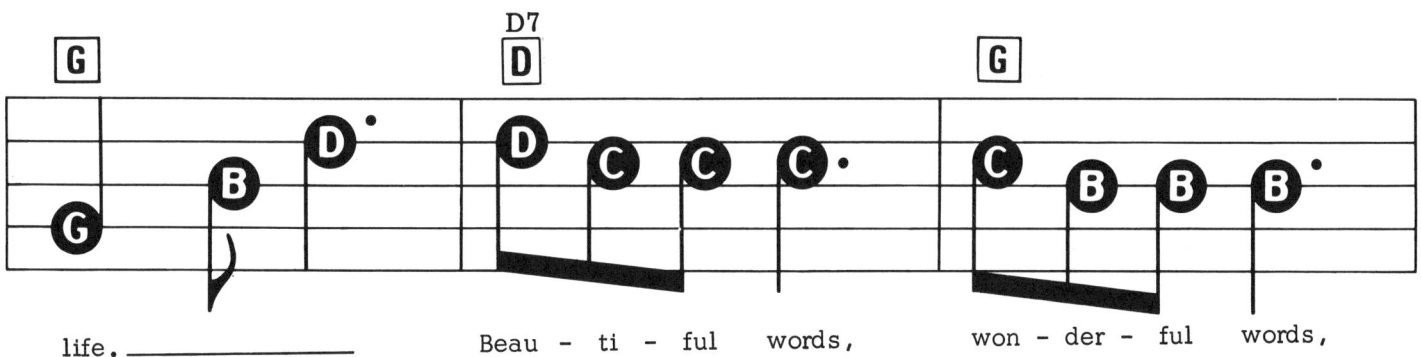
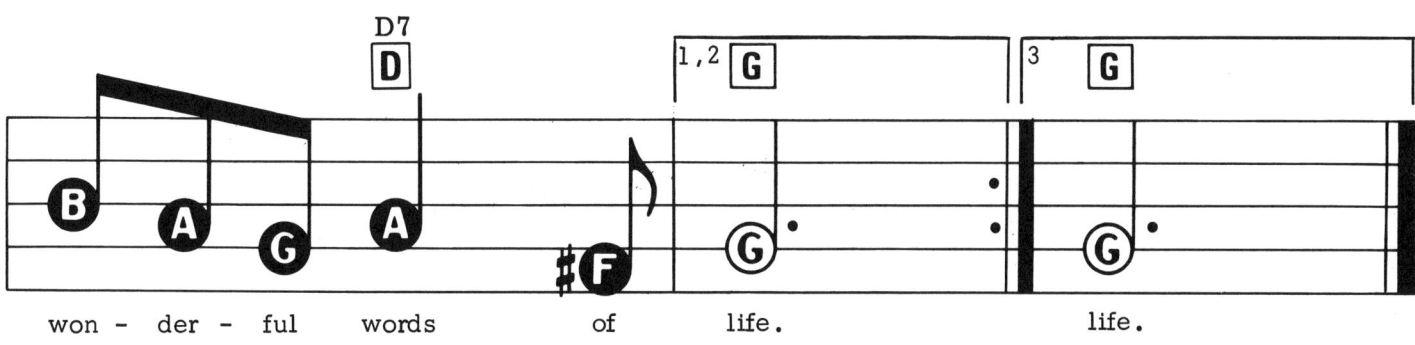

# Registration Guide

- Match the Registration number on the song to the corresponding numbered category below. Select and activate an instrumental sound available on your instrument.
- Choose an automatic rhythm appropriate to the mood and style of the song. (Consult your Owner's Guide for proper operation of automatic rhythm features.)
- Adjust the tempo and volume controls to comfortable settings.

Registration

1	Flute, Pan Flute, Jazz Flute
2	Clarinet, Organ
3	Violin, Strings
4	Brass, Trumpet
5	Synth Ensemble, Accordion, Brass
6	Pipe Organ, Harpsichord
7	Jazz Organ, Vibraphone, Vibes, Electric Piano, Jazz Guitar
8	Piano, Electric Piano
9	Trumpet, Trombone, Clarinet, Saxophone, Oboe
10	Violin, Cello, Strings